Life is limited .... Live Unlimited

SIMPLY, SAFELY, STRONGLY

Sanjiva S. Dubey

BLOOMSBURY

LONDON • NEW DELHI • NEW YORK • SYDNEY

Bloomsbury Publishing India Pvt Ltd
Vishrut Building, DDA Complex
Building No. 3, Pocket C-6 & 7, Vasant Kunj
New Delhi 110 070

ISBN: 978-93-84052-76-8
10 9 8 7 6 5 4 3 2 1

Typeset by Eleven Arts
Printed and bound by Replika Press Pvt Ltd

Life is limited .... Live Unlimited

Dedicated to my parents,
Late Vidyawati Dubey and Late Sidheshwar Dubey

Contents

Preface

The hyper pace of our times, aggressive competitiveness and desire to amass everything almost instantaneously has taken a toll on our lives. This is manifested in unmanageable stress, poor health, emotional breakdowns, physiological problems or just feeling lost in the world. Talk to any bright young professional, matured mid-career executive or professional veterans; majority of them rue that their life could have been better. Most agree in private that the pace of competitiveness and increased consumerism is proving counterproductive and look for simple answers, none of which seem suitable. They struggle to manage their day-to-day chores and tend to lose the larger perspective of their life while taking a roller coaster ride of their career journey. All of them need to strike a balance with life, work and the external environment, before it is too late.

Our life, our most prized possession, is not to be splurged on meaningless pursuits, aimless endeavours and worthless relationships. This is truly a gift of God and must be spent happily, responsibly and purposefully. Neither do the isolated society and trembling family systems provide adequate cushioning from emotional upheavals, financial uncertainties, nor do they provides a sense of security. Nuclear families or single parents who have meagre support from their extended family have very little to connect with their roots. In the event of major disappointments—emotional, career-related, study-related or financial—they take extreme steps to end their life or withdraw into themselves, and while away their time doing nothing. They need a framework, a positive method that can help them adopt a balanced approach to life comprising work, pleasure, family responsibilities and also things that give them a sense of worthiness. Some can find purpose in life by making a hobby their means of living, some in social service, some in research or some in an organisation that they are part of. They also need a simple framework that they can apply to balance various aspects of their life.

How does work life balance of employees help organisations? A well balanced life is a treasure, not only for the employee but for the employers as well. Leading corporations have initiated steps to enable their employees maintains this balance. These enterprises are cognizant of the fact that a well-balanced employee is far more productive, stable team-player and long term asset than a hyper active, dangerously competitive and a damagingly aggressive one. The later may show short term results, but will also vitiate the work environment. Most progressive corporations emphasise, educate and mandate employees to take necessary steps for their work life balance. These efforts include developing policies, creating a climate that respects such initiatives, promoting self-help groups and communities amongst others. They must take these steps to arrest the chaos that we see today of skyrocketing attrition, issues of corruption and increasing work force militancy in developing world. We have a chapter for the employers to take action in this direction.

What will happen if we don't strike a balance? We have seen dangerous consequences for people who fail to balance their work and personal life. Their struggle in the multi-aspirational world is frustrating and confusing. The greed to garner more money or higher status, excessive consumption or lust for sensual pleasure, all of them without moderation is like a bubble that will burst one day. Many promising individuals have decimated too early to become fodder to the breaking news stories. That includes poster boy CEOs as well as stepping in the door youngsters. In contrast there is thousands of silently suffering but rarely complaining professionals who are living their life from one frustration to next depression. They have accepted their life as it comes a day at a time without any desire hope or goal achieving nothing that ultimately matters. All These people need similar treatment for rebalancing their life.

While nursing our career sometimes we tend to forget that our life needs a balanced approach to succeed and be happy. In the interest of career we drop all our other interests, hobbies and at times family and community responsibilities. If we are successful in a way, we pursue the beaten path with punishing doggedness. Come a failure, the extreme frustration, superlative tension and bout of depression engulfs them all. They have no other dimension of life to look up to. The net result is the occasional and disturbing news of extreme steps like drugs, suicide or crime, taken by youngsters, budding professionals or end-of-life celebrities, which comes to us with constant regularity.

Ironically no age group is isolated from such imbalance. From tender teens to twinkling twenty, thriving thirty or fearful forty, funny fifty to surrendered sixty, all ages face such behaviour. Balancing work life habit can not be picked up as a grown up venture but should be inculcated right since the childhood. As the years pass by it becomes tougher to value work life moderation. Enlightened parents advocate balance to their children and advice them not to worry too much when disappointed and avoid too much of elation on their achievements.

The book will help these silent sufferers of work life imbalance to road map from what they are doing to what they should ideally do in their life.

So how do we go about attaining work our life balance? The protagonist of this book is a person of you-and-me variety who realises after a serious life threatening accident, that his life is not just about living in the fast lane but doing something more meaningful and enjoying. He took a resolve to change its course by bringing balance to make it more holistic. The transformation to peace and serenity in his life was achieved through simple self discovery, extensive reading of this subject and picking up practical ideas for implementation. He gradually started to implement these ideas to find phenomenal results. Not only his career satisfaction improved manifold, his life looked more enjoying and family far more comfortable. In the process these ideas have crystallised into an actionable framework that this is book is all about. This book is a culmination of extensive and distilled research of this subject, rigorous experiential trial and arriving at practical wisdom. This book is also an honest confession of accepting why it is not easy to practice what someone preaches.

Suitable for all ages the story gives just one message ***Life is limited ... live unlimited....*** do it Simply, Safely, Strongly.

Sanjiva S Dubey, Guru Punima

Acknowledgements

Every time someone came struggling with the problem of work life imbalance, I wondered how I could share the practices that helped me. However, putting book together on a subject which is a true modern age phenomenon, and impacts the author as much as the reader, was not easy. It was like testing a medicine before prescribing it to someone else. Translating complex principles, practices and learning to easy-to-adopt methods suited to the busy professionals in an easy and practical manner was equally difficult. So I decided to walk the talk before I prescribe it to my fellow professionals.

Much of this journey of writing as well as simultaneous transformation has been witnessed, supported, questioned and encouraged by the immediate family comprising my wife Vibha, son Priyamvad, and daughter Devisha. They want me to improve still and I will, for sure. Without them neither the book nor the author would have survived in his present form. I owe them my life and plead guilty for the delayed start of this journey of my personal transformation.

Many of my colleagues, both from the past and present, especially from IBM, and client organisations like Airtel and many others have stood by me when I needed them most. I am here because of them and my gratitude goes out to each one of these individuals and organisations. I wish to thank my employer IBM and its senior management for supporting my writing pursuits. This organisation is a wonderful place to work especially for the subject around which this book is about. Thanks is also to my numerous colleagues in industry current as well as former who have encouraged me to write my experienced and were ready to be a wily listeners, wanted to try the tips or two and report their results.

My sincere thanks to Bloomsbury Publication, Rajiv Berry, Praveen and the entire team who helped me convert my thoughts into reality.

Above all, I pay my gratitude to God almighty who desired that this work be executed by me. Without the grace of the God almighty none of our efforts could ever be realised. I thank the almighty to have chosen me to tell my friends ... *Life is limited ....Live Unlimited.*

Sanjiva S Dubey
Gurupurnima, New Delhi

About the AUTHOR

Sanjiva S. Dubey has several decades of senior executive experience across several Industries. He is currently Asia Pacific Executive of the IBM global account. In the past, he has held positions such as Country Principal of IBM Consulting, CEO and President and Specialist of Management Development. He has taught as Visiting Professor at IIM Lucknow, Indore and Rohtak and other institutes such as MDI, BIMTECH, XLRI, and NIT Jamshedpur among others. He has written six books including the award-winning *Innovation with IT* He has published over fifty research articles in leading journals. His hobbies include writing on current affairs for newspaper columns and poetry, which he writes under a pen name. He mentors, coaches and advices to a large number of youngsters and peers. Currently, he lives in Delhi with his family. He can be reached at itsm.ssdubey@gmail.com.

CHAPTER ONE

Wake Up LIFE IS LIMITED

It's terrible to realize you don't learn how to live until you're ready to die and, then it's too late.
—Edna Ferber (1887–1968, American author)

The Year that Was

Hotel Okhura, Tokyo, 16th June

The soft music and sound of sea waves emanating from the wall-size plasma screen was creating a soothing effect on him. He was seated on a wide plush chair in the oxygen bar on the 18th floor of Hotel Okhura in Tokyo. It was a rainy June morning and for him this was the most relaxing experience after a hectic schedule since he landed two weeks ago. The wide chair was very comfortable with adjustable legs, head and armrest. The headphones were equally effective, all managed through a convenient remote control embedded in the armrest.

'You may now relax for the next 40 minutes and I will wake you up once done. If you need further assistance, press the attendant button on the remote...' spa attendant softly said after setting the oxygen flow and showing him how to operate the same. He closed his eyes to enjoy the environs.

'Shall I increase the oxygen flow?' the attendant of the oxygen bar, all dressed up in white, asked before stepping out.

'Oh no, it is fine', he replied with his semi-closed eyes. Jeeva was slowly drifting into a state between half asleep and deep slumber. Suddenly he recalled that this was not an unfamiliar question. He was asked the same question nearly a year back on the same date, 16th June, but in an altogether different setting!

He recalled in his dreamy eyes, a lady in a similar white uniform asking the same question, 'Shall I increase the oxygen flow?'

He had by then traveled back in time. The location was different. Yes, he was inhaling oxygen. Lots of people in white uniform were around him. But it was not the oxygen bar of any other spa, but the casualty room of Apollo Hospital in Chennai.

'It hurts ....all over,' he recalled muttering to himself in response to this question when he could barely open his eyes.

'Are you ok?' This time a nurse in white inquired, coming closer to his face.

'It hurts ... I am not able to move my left hand, nor can I turn my body.' He mumbled through the oxygen mask covering his mouth. His own voice sounded different to him, as if coming from a distant land. He could barely see through his heavily sedated eyes. But he knew where he was.

There were people around in the room, none of them he could recognize. He was surrounded by a battery of doctors examining him from various angles and discussing over the X-ray and CT scan reports. There were a dozen gadgets and probes attached to his body to monitor his vital functions. For the attending doctors, he was yet another patient struggling with his life after a serious road accident. For them, it was yet another day, neither better nor worse in any case! But for him, this was a day he will not forget for rest of his life.

There was also a man in khaki[1] amongst the group of doctors and nurses. This man was in no mood to wait. For the last hour or so he was fed up listening to umpteen diagnostic angles. Awaiting the patient's reports, doctors were discussing the case details while monitoring his parameters. The police man could not understand

[1]Khaki is the colour of the uniform of Indian policemen.

most of the medical terms, but he could make out that the patient was in real bad shape. Unless the patient regained his senses soon, it may be too late. The officer knew that in such cases he would have difficulty filing his report to close the case. He was no mood to take up any additional work.

After a while, the patient opened his eyes. The group of doctors were enthusiastic now, more so when the patient mumbled a few words. For the police man, it was a signal to complete his task and rush back to his cup of steaming morning coffee. He asked the doctors, 'May I take his statement?'

The senior doctor advised him to go easy but nonetheless signaled him to proceed. The police officer leaned over Jeeva and asked few questions about him, his address, etc., and finally asked, 'How did it happen?'

'A bus came and hit my car ... Oh it hurts,' he finally spoke up in a slow halting tone.

'Was it the bus driver's fault or the taxi driver's?' the police officer inquired.

'No one's fault.... My bad luck perhaps,' and he tried to smile and closed his eyes.

Then he remembered the following two lines from Ramchartimanas:

हानि लाभ जीवन मरण यश अपयश विधि हाथ[2]

The doctor signaled the end of conversation to the police officer. The officer asked the patient to sign on some paperwork as a testimony to his statement, after which he closed his diary and left the patient's enclosure.

Surprisingly, the patient found that his right hand worked effortlessly while signing the paper!

Has anyone from the family arrived?' One of the doctors asked.

'Yes, they flew in from Delhi last evening. Now they are waiting for your permission to meet the patient,' said the attending nurse.

'Let him stabilise first. Maybe they should meet after an hour or so. Monitor his vitals and report to me in about 45 minutes. If he is stable, allow one or two of the close family members to meet him,'

[2]*Loss or gain, life or death, honour or dishonour are all decided by destiny.*

the senior doctor said. After giving some more instructions, he left along with the team leaving behind the lone nurse in the casualty enclosure with the struggling patient.

While, the patient had closed his eyes and was not able to speak much, he was aware about what was happening around him. Now that he was back to his senses, he realised that his hearing too was perfect. He tried to remember the Mahamrintunjay's mantra[3] of lord Shiva, the savior of all.

ॐ त्र्यम्बकं यजामहे सुगन्धिं पुष्टिवर्धनम् ।
उर्वारुकमिव बन्धनात् मृत्योर्मुक्षीय मामृतात् ।।

Initially, he could only remember a few syllables of this mantra which he was so fluent reciting before the accident. Slowly pushing his memory, he tried reconstructing the remaining part of the mantra. Once he was able to mumble the entire mantra, he felt himself protected—as if Lord Shiva was telling him, 'You will soon get well, don't worry.' Jeeva kept repeating this mantra in his mind.[4]

However, his body was not responding in the same manner as his brain was. He could feel a number of gadgets attached to his idle body. There was a drip attached to one of his arms. He was not able to lift the other arm, which was in a cast with a sling around it. He also occasionally felt himself gasping for breath; as if he was not able to suck enough oxygen into his lungs. It was like a feeling one gets in a polluted environment or at high altitudes. What happened to him in his inner body? He got worried yet he mumbled, 'But I am alive.'

—Ramcharitmanas, Saint Tulsidas.

[3]This is a very powerful and revered mantra, and if chanted with devotion can cure all illness and protect us from diseases. The author has found great faith in it and recommends readers to learn to recite when they need protection from ill-health.

English translation: *OM. Tryambakam Yajamahe, Sugandhim Pushti-vardhanam Urvarukamiva bandhanan Mrityor mukshiya Mamritat.*

[4]Repeating shlokas called *manas-jap*, in one's mind, is a powerful way to derive blessings from God.

'You need something,' the nurse leaned over him with a smile.

He responded in the negative with a faint smile on his face. For the first time he felt he could smile too!

It was the Longest Day

'I am alive and can talk. More importantly, I can think, feel and remember where I am'. His thoughts started to gain control over his senses. It was perhaps 48 hours since he met with the accident and was lying unconscious. A true statement would be that he was not exactly unconscious for the entire duration. He was coming back to his senses in between in spurts. He could occasionally feel himself going through various stages, being lifted in stretcher, shouts of people, being wheeled in Operations Theater or C T Scan table. But he was not able to participate in these activities around him. Once or twice he asked for water and once he did say that his family be called. All these hours he was an observer to himself.

Like most mornings on his travel schedule that day also started at about 4 am. Frequent travel was just a routine for him. He was used to waking up at wee hours and prepare himself for a long rush throughout the day. That day as well he had to catch an early morning flight from the Kamraj Airport in Chennai to Mumbai. He had a series of meetings lined up in Mumbai during the day. Finally, he was to take the last flight back to Delhi, where his family lived. In fact his frequent travel schedule made him quote that he lives out of a suitcase and on the airplane. 'But my family lives in Delhi and I return to them as often as I can, at least at the end of every week!' he would add with a grin.

After finishing his morning rituals, he began his day by lighting an incandescent stick and offering a prayer to Lord Hanuman ji, whose picture he always carried in his travel kit. As he was saying his prayer, the guest house telephone rang to announce the arrival of his taxi. 'I'll be down in a minute,' he said and wrapped up the remaining activities. After keeping all the sundry items in the carry bag, he zipped it up and continued sipping tea.

His dressing up routine even at home was a treat to watch. It was funny for some, but usually invited censure from people who cared. A hyperactive person to the core, he would try to accomplish everything in shortest period of time. An efficiency freak, who will jump out of bed like a spring doll comes to life as soon as its wrapper box is opened. At times he would push the tooth brush in his mouth at the speed of light only to invite frowns from his mother or spouse. In the duration when others would have just taken their first gulp of water, he would have finished the entire toilet ritual. He would run from his bedroom to the living area many times during this process like a speedboat and stuff things in his laptop bag as they are found littered all over his work area. He would shave while sipping tea, keep making calls while dressing up, continue to stuff his mouth while flipping TV channels and also read the morning newspaper alongside. He took great pride in the fact that he could get ready in 20 minutes flat after hearing the first beep of the alarm. He would brag of this feat as if he had just been nominated to the Guinness book of world records.

Finally, when he would leave the home, a trail of objects strewn across the house would be testimony to a recent storm. Be it the used night dress, wet towel, half finished toast or empty tea cup, all these would silently tell as if a hurricane has left travails of destruction.

'Why can't you get up 30 minutes early?' was a sentence he had heard a zillion times since his childhood. Initially it was his mother, then spouse and now his daughter who took turns to admonish him but without effect.

On the fateful day in Chennai he finished his morning rituals pretty quickly. The taxi was parked just opposite the guest house, but on the other side of the road. The guest house attendant kept the travel bag in its boot compartment. 'Give me the laptop bag. I will keep it with me,' he said. Since the passenger side door was too close to the side walk, he decided to sit just behind the driver, keeping his laptop next to him.

Time: 4:30 am.

The taxi started to crawl on the TTK road towards the Chennai Airport. The early morning cab drivers appear as if they are racing against Narayan Kartikeyan in a formula one race. But what can they do otherwise? They generally get their guest roster rather late in the night. Before the last drop of the day and early hour pick up of next morning, they have to go home; mostly in the outskirts of cities. Most drivers start pretty early around 3:30 am and rush to the downtown hotels or guest houses to pick up guests, who themselves rarely come out in time. These drivers drive without speed limits and show scant respect to red lights or other vehicles at these hours.

Meanwhile, Jeeva in the backseat was busy looking at the air ticket jacket to locate the airport tele check-in number. 'Oh I must do the tele check-in, it is already late.' He dialed the number and waited for the response from the other end. Tring... tring.... 'Oh come on lift it up' he said to himself.

Screeeetchh!!! .... Wham!

Suddenly he was jolted by a huge impact and was tossed along with the car several feet up in the air. Almost everything was spinning around him as the car rolled several times while he was sandwiched between the two seats.

He did not remember momentarily what happened soon after. He was in state of complete shock. When he got back his composure a little later, he experienced unbearable pain in his back, gasping for breath, huge urge of thirst and of course shouts of people gathered around the intermingled car and bus combine. But now he cannot do anything he knew pretty well. Others have to!

Delhi, 5:15 am

About 15 minutes later, a cell phone rang beside a lady deep in sleep, hundreds of miles away in Delhi's downtown home. She was just getting into the prettiest hour of sleep, the early morning one. With no school-going children to prepare (vacation time!), her husband on a zip-in zip-out schedule from city to city during the week days, there was no real hurry for her to get up early.

By the time she woke up from slumber, the cell stopped ringing. The cell rang again for a few tones but then it stopped again. This time she decided to look at the missed call log, which said

Two missed calls ... Jeeva.[5]

[5]Who is Jeeva or *Jivatma*? It is you and I, a body with life, give it any name but it is the same. A *Jivatma* is the subtle or astral body, i.e., five basic elements + mind + intellect + ego, in presence of *Atma*, the Divine Witness. For the purpose of our story, this is an imaginary character, but one can be seen amongst us!.

'Why is he calling repeatedly this early?' She thought.

Jeeva was supposed to be back from Chennai via Mumbai as per his earlier schedule. Normally, whenever she didn't pick up the cell phone, he would send a sweet short message to which she would reply later.

'Has his plan to go to Mumbai changed and he is coming back to Delhi instead?' She assumed that he may have wanted to tell the driver to come early to pick him up at the airport. 'Or has he forgotten to say something and wanted me to attend it during the day? Strange are these business development consultants' schedule,' she murmured!

She decided to call him back while massaging her sleepy eyes and dialed on her phone.

After a few rings someone picked up the cell phone. She heard unfamiliar background noise and shouts but surprisingly not the familiar voice of Jeeva, yet she said 'Hello...'

'Helooo. Helooo madam…' an unfamiliar voice spoke from the other end.

Who is this? She wondered.

'Accident madam, please talk to Sir,' the same voice responded.

'Hello … I am hurt. Met with a serious car accident … just now... I can't talk much.' Jeeva was gasping for breath but continued in his halting tone. 'Please call someone in the office to attend to me. I am lying on the street. Speak to the driver for location.' Jeeva spoke very slowly as if in great pain. Then he passed on the phone to the driver.

'What happened? Where is he?' she asked the driver repeatedly.

'Madam. Chennai, TTK Road, major accident, pain, inner injury, very bad madam, very bad … taking hospital.' The cab driver on the other side was speaking partly in Tamil and partly in broken English, barely making sense. And then the line got disconnected. She rushed out of bed. 'Oh God! Jeeva has met with an accident,' she said to herself.

She ran straight to the telephone desk and fumbled with the telephone diary. In the days of personal mobile phones, ironically she had no numbers of Jeeva's office colleagues in her cell phone. The poor old desk telephone diary came to her rescue. Finally, she located a number to Jeeva's office colleague. She decided that in future she would certainly store numbers of Jeeva's colleagues and also of their children's friends in case of such emergencies. But that will be done later.

Back in Chennai, while still waiting for the rescue team to arrive, Jeeva was feeling unbearable pain in his back and was unable to breathe properly. While he was not bleeding profusely, something with his chest seemed to have gone wrong. He was entering a bout of unconsciousness, and felt like dozing off.

Kamraj Airport, Chennai: Departure Lounge

5:30 am, As soon as Vinay stepped into the security area, his cell rang.

'Hello,' he responded.

'Vinay… this is Arpi…. Jeeva has met with an accident on … his wife called up just now.'

'Oh! Where did it happen? That is why I didn't see him at the airport while checking in. Is his cell working?' Vinay asked.

'Just half an hour ago, while on his way to the airport, TTK Road…. Yes his cell is working…. Can you rush to the accident site and attend to him please…'

Meanwhile, the security staff was getting annoyed with the continued conversation. Vinay took back his boarding pass from the security staff and rushed outside to catch a cab.

The longest day had just begun for all those who cared for Jeeva. But by then Jeeva was unconscious.

Apollo Hospital, Greames Road Chennai, 17th June

A day later, Jeeva came back to his senses, mumbling few sentences, but unable to move his body. Immobile with multiple fractures in his body, he could only talk and that too in-coherently.

'Are you feeling better?' Dr Vijay Shankar, the cardio-thoracic surgeon asked him during his morning rounds a couple of days later.

'Yes, I feel better. What is the damage, doctor?' Jeeva wanted to know.

'Oh you have fractured your scapula, and 8 out of 12 ribs,' he said while looking at the X-ray plate. 'But these will heal over time, nothing to worry, though there will be pain for some time. We will make an incision into your spinal cord to alleviate the pain by dripping medicines directly.' He smiled and paused as if contemplating whether to give the next news to him or not. 'The only worry is that your left lung has totally collapsed. While we are giving pressurised oxygen to make you comfortable, you have to slowly return to normal breathing, as otherwise the body will get conditioned to the external feed. So continue to breathe through the mask but in between attempt to breathe of your own as much as you can. This is the only way we can take you out of the life support system. Regarding your head injury, the neurophysician will advice you the necessary medication and precautions to follow. Similarly, the requisite care that is needed for the all bone injuries will be explained by the orthopedic surgeon. One more thing, the physiotherapist will start visiting you after 2 days. He will help you to start moving your limbs, etc.' Dr Vijay Shankar paused and then said slowly smiling at him, 'You will be normal. Not to worry.'

'Doctor, how long will it take for me to get back to work? I am a busy person?' He mumbled with anticipation.

The doctor laughed at his 'busy' statement but said, 'Well it depends on the recovery process. A couple of months, if not years. But I must tell you, you are very lucky,' and walked away with a smile.

Doctors have a very difficult task to enthuse confidence in seriously ill patients, and Dr Vijay Shankar was doing exactly that, albeit effortlessly.

'Sir, the car was so badly damaged, if one could see it, no one would believe that the occupants would have survived.' Vinay told him when he came to see Jeeva later in the day. Vinay added, '.You are very lucky. You are safe, that is what the doctors are saying.'

Few months later when he was showing the discharge report to his regular physician, Dr Kohli, he looked at all the reports and said, 'You are very lucky. You are alive and that is a miracle.'

Back to Hotel Okhura, Tokyo, 16th June, A Year Later

'I am indeed very lucky,' Jeeva mumbled and thanked God for not only his recovery but for necessary wisdom to rework his life's priorities in the past twelve months.

'Did you say something?' inquired the spa attendant.

'Oh nothing, just take off the mask please,' Jeeva said to the lady.

'You mean the oxygen tube?' The lady attendant asked politely.

Jeeva looked around. There was no hospital, no ICU, but the plush surrounding of Hotel Okhura.

'Oh yes. Can you take off the tube please,' he said and got off the elevated sofa. After leaving oxygen bar, he rushed to his hotel room to prepare for his next meeting with invited CEOs later in the day. Life was back to normal but with a difference for him.

While inhaling oxygen, Jeeva travelled back in time and re-lived the frightful past year in 15 minutes. It had been exactly a year since he met with that massive accident. The recovery process was an uphill and challenging task, but he could achieve it with a lot of support from his friends and family. Someone who was not able to get up on his own few days after the accident, who was unconsciously wheeled inside the hospital just a year ago on this very day, has finally returned to work, and normally.

After a year since that incident he was following almost the same work schedule with equal intensity but in totally different manner. The new found realisation of reworking his life's priorities and finding new meaning in his work changed his approach. He now strived to balance his life beyond his career, material possession and worldly achievements on those things that have started to give him new meaning, purpose of life and above all peace of mind. He had already made significant changes and was going on with a renewed vigour to make this change happen in his life. He knew that life is too short to be wasted brooding over past happenings or on incessant contemplation for the future, but in living happily in the present which is so precious.

The year that had gone by made him realise a new vision for himself, for his life and his work. He was now better equipped to prioritise what he wanted in his life. He now became more choosy about his role and career options. He became much more aware about how much work to bite into and what to strive for in his life. More importantly, he knew what not to accept and not to regret afterwards. In his day to day life he was better prepared to decide what work to do and when. In addition he was clear what he should not do and why. He also felt he became more assertive, strong and enjoyed his new found success, the definition which is now changed.

After a year since the unfortunate event, he does not muse over refusing opportunities that he feels do not fall in the line of his goals. He is not easily influenced by people's opinion now as he used to be in the past. Aping others either voluntarily, by cajoling or inducement were things of past for him. At work he became more organised and efficient. He was less pushy but was able to achieve more through his proactive planning, mentoring and delegation. He gathered more peace and tranquility around himself. This resulted in spreading his wings to take up more responsibilities, albeit cross functional, creative and value adding to himself and to the organisation. He improved his visualisation for impending problems and thus could take efforts to prevent or minimise them, leading to accolades from his superiors.

Finally, he realised that like everyone else his life too had a limited span. He must, therefore, spend every minute of it wisely. This wake up call really helped him to start every day with renewed vigour and a sense of purpose. He simply reworked his life balance when an inner voice said: Wake up Jeeva, life is limited!

Summary of the Key Theme

Most people who go through such life-threatening situations learn one or two lessons.

Jeeva too had a few.

1. He felt that his life has several untouched dimensions that need to be valued equally along with his career and worldly possessions. His immobile body had nothing else to do but think as it was recuperating. A year-long introspection helped him dig deeper into various philosophical and spiritual literature along with contemporary research on the subject of the inner meaning of life, work, and physical health and related subjects to find an answer. It led him to develop an approach for himself, which he practiced over several months. Surprisingly to his worldly, analytical and logical mind, he felt that these worked!
2. He practiced the art of prioritisation in his life, science of planning and delegation for his work and developed better chemistry with

people around him. He knew that like him, many others were also going through similar challenges. This accident served as a wakeup call for him to truly invigorate his life. After practicing some of these principles, he could steal enough time to think about what is not working well in his life and how could he correct these aspects.

Our readers, however, need not wait for such events to kick-start thinking about the issue of work life balance. They need not travel all the roads to know what pitfalls and problems are in store for them. They can prepare for work life balance using experiences of friends like Jeeva and many others. This way they can prevent losing their precious time in life before they ultimately discover their own datum.

A balanced work life helps us prevent aimless wandering for unrealistic goals, encourages valuing relationships and overcomes frustration of failures. It also nudges us to slow down when life seems unbelievably good. When life is well balanced only then can a person end up creating a purpose for himself. Life is a beautiful gift from God and it must be lived happily, purposefully and responsibly. It also means that we need to balance its various aspects, and take steps to achieve them. Let us not value those things that we do not have or value them only when they are lost. Let us start valuing them when we possess them. Our life is one such precious one!

मीत समझ में आये कैसे वस्तु पास मेरे रहती जो
चाहे हों सम्बन्ध सुरीले या फिर अपना ही जीना भी
जो कुछ पास नहीं वे लगते मिल जाते तो कितने अच्छे
पर वे नहीं कभी कुछ देते हों अलभ्य वस्तु कितना भी

...... सशंदु[6]

That was the lesson that Jeeva learnt … the hard way.

[6]Oh my friend I never realised your worth when you were with me, never valued all relationships including my own life because they were with me. Hankered repeatedly for those things that were not with me. They may be good but never gave anything to me.

CHAPTER TWO

Analyse to REALISE

Life is what happens to you, while you're busy making other plans.

—John Lennon.

Back to the ICU, 16th June, A Year Earlier

Most of those days, while lying alone in the hospital bed, Jeeva would play with his own thoughts, tossing and turning them around. His body was immobile, hurting all around as if he was soaked in a tub full of pain. However, he could think painlessly going over his past life and contemplating what future could have in store. It was a long summer afternoon when quiet descends in empty hospital corridors forcing even the attending nurse to take a quick nap. Jeeva started to replay in his head the day of his accident that he did not witness.

What would have happened to his work afterwards?

He went on to reconstruct the day of the accident in his imagination. He was supposed to meet the CEO of a prominent customer in Mumbai that day but that was not to be.

What would have happened to the meeting?

How did the meeting go?

Were those issues that he was supposed to address, resolved?

There was a crisis in the project. The customer's CEO was unhappy and had escalated the outstanding issues to the senior management of his company. That is why Jeeva was asked to step in to take charge of the situation and douse the fire.

'Only you could do it Jeeva,' said his manager who asked him to take multicity tour at a short notice. Now that he was lying incapacitated what would have happened to the meeting without him? He was truly worried.

But after a few moments another thought came to him rather brutally that the meeting would have happened without him any way, and as planned!

He started to reconstruct the hypothetical situation of the day that had already passed without his knowledge. He just transposed himself invisibly to the 16th floor Cuff Parade office of the client on the fateful 16th June morning. All the invitees would have assembled in the board room, but without him. His colleagues from Mumbai would have shown helplessness due to Jeeva's absence. They would have by then conveyed the news of his accident, albeit seriously to all present in the board room. Everyone present would have regretted the unforeseen happening, nevertheless.

'How is he?' The client's CEO would have asked after entering the room.

Jeeva was well known to him. Being a nice individual himself, the CEO would have certainly thanked God that Jeeva was safe and recuperating. Everyone would have inquired a bit more about the accident. Collectively the assembled gathering would have blamed the lorry driver or that of his car, shown frustration about the decreasing road safety, sighting recent statistics and even blamed traffic police or government, not necessarily in the same order. But after a few sentences of sympathy, the agenda must have been put up on the screen. Someone must have stepped in to present 'Jeeva's presentation' and do 'his assignment' as best as possible.

Similarly, his team behind at the Delhi office would have started the day with a shock after hearing the news. They would have gathered to exchange more information and assigned some folk to help his family. Finally, the impending work would have taken away the brewing anxiety from his colleagues' minds. After some time, they would have resumed their work with deep sympathy for him. Yet, his close family and colleagues would have continued to keep a round-the-clock vigil as he was inching back to normal. The rest of the world would have decided to move on.

'Close family and colleagues are keeping a close watch and vigil.' He repeated these words in his mind as he whispered in the oxygen mask. How could he think the entire world would have stopped without him? This assumption is absolutely wrong. The world does not stop for any one however great or mighty he may be!

The world would not have stopped without him!

An idle body and sound mind is a deadly combination for thinking the unthinkable.

Jeeva's problem-solving mind was by then aroused to find an answer to this question. Granted that the world would not have stopped without him but *what would have really stopped without him, if at all*?

He needed to find the answer to this important question to ascertain the importance of his presence in this world. In his thoughts he drew the problem solving fish bone,[1] a diagram with several major threads of the likely causes. A typical problem solving diagram would have causes categorised under people, process, and technology and strategy area, but in a real-life situation the likely causes would be different. He continued to be probed further.

If he is not around, his family will surely miss him. So will his colleagues at work. His office will also feel a void due to his absence. May be the society, community or nation too would miss him as a useful contributor. He knew well that depending upon the stage and state of the life one belongs to, the importance of each of these voids will vary.[2] If you are a young professional, your family will surely miss

[1]Also called Ishikawa diagrams (or cause-and-effect diagrams) that show the cause and effect of a certain problem.

[2]A person of eminence will have a large share of his self towards society, nation, etc. Even all of us, however ordinary we may be, do and could contribute towards our society or nation. Several simple persons have turned out in times of

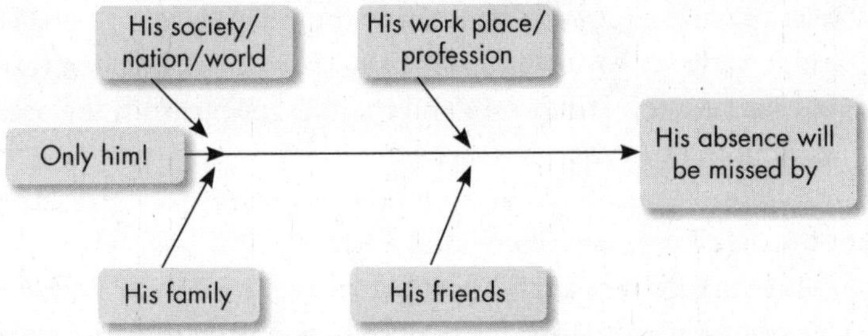

Figure 2.1 A person is missed by...

you as you may be the sole bread winner of the family, but that may not be the case when you are past your prime and have grown-up children. Yet, if you are doing extensive community service, or working for a national cause, a larger section of the society would miss you.

He dwelled in detail what all will be missed in his absence, especially in the work area:

- *His work output?* But someone else can easily step in.
- *His own glory for having reached a high rank in the hierarchy of his organisation?* Who cares after some time for all the 'former' rank holders? Even mighty kings are relegated to history, who cares for an ordinary engineer and MBA?
- *Loss of a good professional to his company?* Well, the hiring process would suitably replace the vacancy sooner or later.
- *Loss to society/nation or professional fraternity?* He was just too small to make an impact at larger society or nation level. He had nothing significant on his shoulders to boast about. Even the professional fraternity is too fragile to remember a near-same profile. You be a CEO or a project manager, there are always others to step into your shoes effortlessly. He was no Vishveshswariya, Homi Bhaba, JRD Tata, Ramanujam, Einstein, or likes, whose professional absence is missed for a long time. He was like the hordes of professionals who appear on the scene

crisis and have contributed and saved the society from catastrophes. It could be just be an ordinary police man who bears the hail of bullets to catch the 26/11 terrorist alive. Or it could be a village lad who runs to towards the running train, waving his red short to inform a broken track to save hundreds of life year after year, perform reasonably for their organisation. They add few zeroes to the balance sheet of the firm, create a team, and nurture few businesses and then disappear from the scene without making their absence felt.

Ironically, he realised that no one in his work space, society or nation would have missed him after a while.

This saddened him a bit. This ugly yet realistic fact of his life, in fact for all such persons like him, made him probe this thought further in a characteristic consultant style of questioning.

So if that hypothesis is true, what next?

He turned his inquiry towards the emotional area of his life covering family and friends. He was sure that the family and friends would miss him definitely a bit longer than his office colleagues, society or the nation. He had a habit of seeing the obituary page of the morning newspaper and noting a thing or two. Most notices refer to recent demise put forward by the grieving family for invitation to the final prayer. Some also use it as subtle publicity of 'XYZ group of companies' for the *karmyogi*[3] who just passed away. Few of them mention beautiful lines quoted from Gita, Bible or a Hindi poetry. All these insertions do recall departed individuals especially young individuals who passed away untimely leaving a void in the lives of the family members and how they miss them and think that the departed soul is guiding them or is around.

Jeeva used to feel that he was a bit different. He was a self-made man like most of the people around, who first constructed a step of their career ladder and then climbed it without much assistance. Not only was he the sole earning member of his family with responsibilities of teenage his children, he also had no great wealth or family lineage to boast of. While money may not pose a constraint to his family due to various provisions made so far and also through organisational support in such cases, his family would definitely miss him on every occasion. All our family members and friends who are no more, do live in our thoughts and keep coming back, for sure.

[3]One who devotes his life to work.

Yet any absence of anyone gets filled over time, albeit slowly. The world would return to its own pace. The show would continue to go on, despite someone not being around. As he continued with these thoughts of his own dispensability, he looked at his immobile torso and felt sad and said to himself 'Oh, Siddhartha (Gautam Budhha) was not wrong when he visualised the transientness of the human life and its continued sufferings during its tenure. A saint like him could renounce his kingdom and search for the true life leaving behind young wife and small child. But he can't even do that without a kingdom'.

Inadvertently two drops flowed out, one from his each eye.

The nurse by the time had woken up from her cat nap, and opened her eyes. She got up and came near him, leaned over and said *are you all right*? Jeeva smiled and nodded in affirmative. Then she wiped those two droplets with the towel kept near his pillow. The nurse was not surprised to see a smile and the tears at the same time. She was used to seeing a plethora of human emotions at her work place and went back to fill her hourly observation charts.

Strangely, Jeeva suddenly realised that it was he, only he who would have missed the unique value of his life the most!

But he was not dead. He was still alive which meant God had given him yet another chance to value his own life. Now he cannot continue living while being a burden on others with an immobile body without any apparent use. That would be too unwelcomed a situation at this stage of his life. Not only he needs his life for himself but he also needs it for his family, friends and larger community. His life story is yet not over and hence he has to make efforts conclude it happily.[4]

He remembered an old story of a highway robber called Ratnakar, who was once confronted with a similar question about his life and its priorities. This question asked by Sage Narad was the starting point for Ratnakar to transform into a renowned saint and poet ultimately. In a different context Jeeva was also about to transform himself too asking a similar question about his life and its priorities.

[4]In the Hindi movie Om Shanti OM, the hero Sharukh Khan has this thought reflected in the dialogue "पिक्चर अभी बाकी है मेरे दोस्त " The show is yet not over !

Story: Only you are responsible for your acts

Ratnakar[5] was a dreaded robber who used to take away belongings of the travelers. As the story goes, he tried once to rob sage Narad. Known for his witty comments, sage Narad asked him a simple question, 'Before you rob off my veena (a musical instrument) and the little that I carry, may I know why you indulge into this crime?' Ratnakar paused for a moment but pat came his answer. 'Swami, I do all this to feed my family like many other do other jobs.' Maharshi Narad said in his characteristic style, 'Narayan, Narayan, I can understand that. But since this an act of crime you will be called sinner. Does the family also share the sin you are amassing, in the similar way they share booty for their survival?' Ratnakar answered that he believes that the family is an equal party to his sin as they are to his booty. Sage Narad then advised him, 'Why not double check up and tell them clearly that what they enjoy is nothing but wealth arising out of robbery!' Ratnakar left Sage Narad tied with a tree and went back to his family to check what they consider his acts as. But he got the utter surprise of his life when his entire family disowned being part of his sin! The family said it was Ratnakar's job to feed for them and they were no way concerned or responsible, to have any share in his sins.

Ratnakar realised his illusion that spending his life for his family doing things that are not ethical and legal, without realising that all acts of omissions and commissions have to be owned by him and him alone. This disenchantment led Ratnakar to worship God as per the advice of Sage Narad. Ratnakar turned to spirituality, became a devoted saint and meditated for many years to earn his name Valmiki. Valmiki was the first poet who wrote the epic Ranmayan.

[5]Saint Valmiki is said to be the original poet who wrote epics like The Ramayana in Sanskrit.

Most of us are Valmiki of our own making. We keep doing things for the rest of the world, family and friends, organisations where we work and for others. Right or wrong we follow a set motion day after day, week after weeks, without realising that in the day-today struggle our own life disappeared serving all others[6]. We pass our days without any purpose, possibilities or something unique to get remembered for. Then comes a day when one realises that he has no life of his own or a very little is left now. While taking care of the rest of the world we forget to take care of the most important person, that is, ourselves.

Jeeva recalled a song he has heard in his childhood days. The opening line of this song said that once you leave your body, no one accompanies you for long. While the wife goes up to the door, friends and family take you to the funeral pyre, and the rest of the journey is carried along with your own *dharm*[7] that you may have accumulated during your life.[8]

This hard truth that no one else can have greater value of the life than the person whose life is at stake, descended on him. Ironically all these thoughts were propelling Jeeva to live his life more holistically and that too with a renewed vigour. He was a non-believer in quitting and always an ardent supporter of living the life fully. Now that he realised that it is he who has to worry about himself, he resolved to put it back on track, starting with his health. His desire to rejuvenate his health became stronger with every breath he took and every mantra he recited while lying on the hospital bed.

'I will get back into shape and will not perpetually depend on my near and dear ones,' he resolved. He must re-work his life that God has given back to him. He must re-orient and recharge his career and re-orchestrate his efforts for his work life balance.

[6]A popular gazal by कृष्ण बिहारी 'नूर' (Krishna Bihari 'Noor'): ज़िन्दगी से बड़ी सज़ा ही नहीं, और क्या जुर्म है पता ही नही, इतने हिस्सों में बट गया हूँ मैं, मेरे हिस्से में कुछ बचा ही नहीं।

There is no more punishment than life, I don't know any other crime than life, and I am cut in so many pieces that no piece is left for me.

[7]Good deeds.

[8]रे मन ये दो दिन का मेला रहेगा, अकेला ही आया है अकेला चलेगा, कायम ये जग का झमेला रहेगा।

It is my life... Why are you bothered?

Most of the time we hear this assertion, from young people who splurge their life in mindless enjoyment, unnecessary speed to race ahead or to gather goodies to in-gratify themselves. Once achieved, they throw away the one in their possession and then look for something anew. The exhilaration of material acquisition is as transient a pleasure as the drag of cigarette smoke in our lungs. It gives a momentary kick but cannot be kept forever. These people proudly say that it is their wish to consuming intoxicants or just pursue material goals without limits. They claim that it is their life and therefore have every right to in gratify, splurge or corrode it at their will. Similarly those running after material success while hastily climbing corporate ladder or pursuing business results with equal doggedness, end up with similar state of momentary pleasure with disastrous consequences ultimately. All short term pleasure has most painful long term results.

Jeeva was fortunate that he belonged to neither of these categories. He was a plain simple middle class boy, who was nurtured with care by his parents imbibing family values and healthy traits. He was liked by his family, favorite of his friends, teachers and colleagues alike. While he would not claim that he is the best looking guy around who will strike an awe with his presence or a serious student of record holder variety, he was just fine, nice in nature, normal and natural. Call it the guy next door within whom you can see your own reflection in varying degrees.

'I am like the common man you see in the R.K. Laxman cartoons everyday in *The Times of India,*' he would joke about himself. But before those who only hear him or have never met him and visualise him wearing check shirt and dhoti as in the cartoon, he would clarify his disposition. 'I am an average Indian 5 ft and 6 inches tall, with round face, a slightly balding forehead, short mustache, wearing a less-than-trendy pair of spectacles who usually dons white shirts with sober ties, dark suits or trousers on formal occasions. However, you can also find him in a plain T-shirt and light coloured trousers on weekends!'

But why was I wearing pink shirt on the day of the accident?

This was a new shirt he reluctantly purchased after being nudged by his wife to try something colourful. 'Was this the cause of his accident?' a voice rose in his head. His thoughts continued to wonder to ascertain reasons of his accident in super natural coincidence and occult messages. His then thought about unlucky date, prohibited direction of travel and on what else could have been the bad omen that caused it. Like many of us he too was haunted by predictions, prophesies and pundits when things do get wrong. We all blame our luck, date, day or the innocent cat that just crossed our path. Was it due to his new shoe; his disturbed brain strayed to suggest.

But soon a good sense prevailed and he brushed aside these wondering thoughts. He recalled that the credit card bill was still to be paid for the shoe and the shirt's purchase. He made a mental note to tell this to his wife to drop a check in time so as not incur any interest. Coming out of his superstitious confabulation on the causes of his accident, he decided that now onwards he will not often talk how, why or when this accident happened. He did not want to behave like many who parrot their physical problem with minutest detail over and over again till they start enjoying them.

What is important in the life?

Now that he has found a new found purpose of his life, that is to balance it, recharge it and rejuvenate it, he directed his thoughts towards actions for the future. He pooled his energy to find things that were important to him, that he must do, attend to or undergo, henceforth.

- What all in his life only he would miss due to his absence, which others would not?
- Are these things worth lounging for?
- What all did he like to do most?
- Can he now start doing them?

These were a few questions he put to himself as he continued thinking.

When he probed further he did come out with not many such desires. Some of it was related to his career achievements, many were also related to his constructive hobbies and some pure recreational ones. No one else perhaps will be interested in them other than him. For instance, his idea of writing a engaging story or a unique business venture is only his desire that many may not be shared by others.

He went back to his childhood days to dig out some of those hobbies. Childhood memories and activities are the fondest for most us. These are the days when we find pleasure in a kite, butterfly or just simple toys. He dusted those young dreams which went awry during his growing up years. 'Can I live them again now that I have been given another chance to live? …' he thought. His responsibilities and desire to do something in life has forgotten this curious child within almost completely. Who will pursue his hobbies that he picked up during the growing up years but could not do justice due to his punishing schedule? He closed his eyes to listen to the inner voice that was relentlessly telling him.

- What will happen to all those songs that he wanted to sing while playing his newly acquired keyboard along with his son? And the ones he wanted to compose and play along the Guitar with his daughter?
- Who will finish his unfinished poetries, articles ideas he wanted to write?
- Who will do justice to his whole library of books that were yet to be read?
- There were several stories in his mind that were yet not written and needed to be shared in a published form.
- What will happen to all these activities, who will do them in his absence?
- He wanted to go on a world tour with his family to all the exotic places that he has seen in movies or in glossy magazines. Those exotic places were still calling him.
- He wanted to set up a self-help group for strugglers like him and also on old age home.

If he is no more, he would definitely miss the precious moments that he wanted to spend with his family. He would miss the joy of enriching his son with his wisdom as he would start to work. He would be deprived of counseling his daughter to take right choice of career. Who will build the school he wanted to, in the name of his parents? He had already thought a suitable name *Sidhesh Vidyalaya* that encompasses both his parents' name. Who will do all this important activities? Not his employer, not his friends or the country/society but it will be he who has to take the cudgel to realise all these dreams.

The list of unrealised cherished desires was getting longer when he included his extended family, friends and colleagues. He realised that he would also miss sharing his anecdotes to his younger folks who just flock around him listen to a new and earthy ones. Most of his anecdotes were found to be full of wisdom by them to clear their *cobwebs of confusion*. He was aware of the sparkle his narration creates in the eyes of its listener. His words have undoubtedly great power to seed unimaginable yet creative thoughts in the minds of its readers and listeners. The list was getting longer and longer of what all personal contribution and creation could have been, if and only if he lives his life his own way. All this were possible provided he was around, alive and kicking and doing his life that is not at the mercy of others.

Ironically, not a single work related responsibilities occurred to him for a moment where his absence would be felt!

He realised that he was dispensable for the world, even to his work place but indispensable to his family, friends and most importantly to himself. He still has to cover a vast uncharted area of his interest and desires that have not been addressed so far in his life. He has simply never attempted doing enough. So far he just focused on his career, work, money and material pursuit, that's all. How can he just leave all these tasks and those towards his family and friends unattended?

This accident has left a deep scar on his physical fitness. The situation after the event was badly staring on his face. How can he work normally with only one functioning lungs out of his two, 8 out of 12 broken ribs, head injury, fractured scapula...etc., etc., and many other problems that doctors have told him not to worry about!

He concluded that in order to bring back his life, his first priority was to recuperate to gain complete body fitness. Only then he can correct the mistakes he has done and take actions with renewed priority. For example, in his earlier disposition he was a non-believer in the strict exercise routine. 'Natural fitness' was his mantra. To support his theory he would claim ancient folklore where tribes used to live on tree tops. 'Our ancestors never went to a gym or jogging track to remain fit so why should we?' He was like most non-descript mid career executives, a non-iron-pumping, non-golfing variety, who live thousand miles below the glass ceilings. He always claimed that if he is able to maintain a tiring routine of physical activities it should be a testimony of his fitness. Lately he added a long evening walk, thinking that it should be enough as far as the physical exercises are concerned. Happy he was with his physique and mandatory yearly checkups till then but not any more. But now he was in a pathetic situation by any standards.

After thinking over several days, he developed a deep resolve to get back to 'shape 1' condition as described by the army fitness protocol. Suddenly, he took off the oxygen mask with one free hand and said, 'let me breathe normally'. The nurse came rushing to him and put the mask back in place.

Besides health all was not well on other dimensions of his work life.

He realised that he was playing with a fire that would have engulfed him anyway, sooner than later. He was running after deadlines after deadlines, targets after target, without any reprieve. Call it living a life in the fast lane that is lived by copying others and dictated by others. There was no time for activities that he liked, loved or lounged.

For instance, he was subjected to endless emails to read and respond. Every other minute his blackberry will blink to announce the arrival yet another email or message. All these emails were a task created by others and copied to several more to read, comprehend, delete or archive. He would get nearly 200+ of them everyday, not to mention several dozens others in his personal email box send by few friends but mostly by greedy marketers. Even if he spends few seconds each to delete them every day, think of the precious minutes these junk mails were stealing from his life. Very clearly he needed to conserve his time from every useless activity to make it available to do things that he wanted to. Time wasting activities like being members of several industry forums, subject matter groups and social networking sites needs to be curtailed to allow him to put back these hours in the areas of his choice.

So far he thought that work is his only priority of his life ... but the life is beyond his work, he now realised it very well.

He recalled those endless week days when he was away from home and those late evenings when he did not return home in time. He missed children interaction while they grew up. Perhaps, he was too concerned for his own career, like many others at this age group. It was rather selfish of him. By spending long hours, and being pliable to receive extra load, he thought his career will shape up. It really did to some extent but at what cost? He was one of the prime examples of a person living just only for work and career. He realised the hard way that the real meaning of his life is beyond work routine.

Talking to the self helps

> *'Thinking' said the little boy 'is when your mouth stays shut and head keeps talking to itself. .. Arkanas Baptist*[9]

Tao had said once, 'learn to return to yourself', and Jeeva learnt that having quiet time helps. All these days while lying on the hospital bed, he was incessantly talking to himself. Call it 'thinking' that we don't do these days often because most of time we are talking to someone or we are being talked to. We all know that the only person with whom we can talk honestly is our own self. A realisation descended that this forced solicitude is helping him to reassess his life. It was also helping him to plan and prioritise for the balance of his life. Jeeva decided that in future he will set aide some time as frequently as possible to get engrossed in his thought while talking to himself. 'I will now take off few days or hours every week doing

[9]Star Teller, Feb 2010, page 1, Publisher The express Newsletter.

just nothing by talking to myself, I think I should,' he agreed to himself and nodded. The nurse looked at him with amusement and offered some water to drink.

Work and Life: Are these together or separate?

Work is not the entirety of our life, so we should not to be spent it just for the 'work' alone. There are several examples of workaholic personalities who develop this 'only-work' profile. Some of them do out of pleasure, at times under duress and end up treating their home as a night shelter. Jeeva was also no different than these people for whom home meant dinner, bed, and breakfast and laundry services.

There is surely something amiss in his life, he thought, but how to crack this work life puzzle? His incapacitate body with super active mind was giving him some unique insight on this subject. He was constantly thinking to find a right balance between work and life. He realised that achieving work/life balance is a continuous process. It is neither one time exercise nor a destination where you can reach sooner or later and be contented with. One has to continuously try, day in and day out. Then a metaphor hit his mind.

Work and life, are like a pair of feet

Can we walk with one foot? Perhaps not! Both feet are necessary to walk and should be equally strong and healthy. Jeeva recalled when he had fractured his knee how difficult it was to manage with just one leg. Even two crutches could not replace his other fractured leg for several months.

Have you noticed that when we walk, the feet have to alternate the weight of the body between each foot? Sometimes we keep weight on one, rest the other but then return on the next one. This is how one moves. Similarly in our life we must give emphasis on work related engagement and non-work related actions, alternatively. We must give each of them the desired time and attention. While it is not denying that work is important to earn our living but there is something important as well beyond the work. While engrossed in our work we should not miss the other side of life…our very larger purpose of life.

We are in Exciting times? Not really!

In the current world we get pushed to do things by others. We have umpteen demands on our time and energy to deliver various expectations. We also want to achieve everything in shortest possible time. A recent TV commercial shows a boy of 6 years booking a car for himself when he will become Vice President at the age of 23 and CEO at the age of 28.

What will he do afterwards?

We don't know how to integrate our work duties, physical well being, spiritual pursuit and social tasks. We get perplexed, overwhelmed and remain confused through out our life. It appears that 'enough' is not enough for most people these days. Everyone wants more within a shortest possible time that too without going through the rigor and grind. Children are borne adult and are subject to compete on ever shifting targets no sooner than they start to walk and talk. The expectations from self and others hold no bar. Consumerism forces us to consume and throw everything. This behaviour continues when we consume and throw our days, months / years and finally our life, without any significant contribution, purpose or achievements. We like stuffing breakfast in our mouth to rush to go to work, take speed lunch to catch up with the next meeting and take dinner while talking on our mobile, watching TV or in a crowded noisy restaurant in absolute chaos. We do not relish every moments we life as it happens to us. Even though we could buy almost every other object available in shops, the novelty wears off as soon as their wrapper is opened and it occupies a place in our crowded home. You call it exciting times; to me it is just sheer madness to live!

The same is true with the way we maintain our relationships. On one hand we send hundreds of SMS to our friends and relatives on the occasion like Diwali or New Year's Day. This is just because it is customary or in-thing to do so. Yet we don't get time for weeks to call up our sisters, cousins and uncles, months to reach out to our ex colleagues and several years to our school or college friends. Frankly, many of us may not have just one person whom we can reach without any hesitation at any hour. Be it a prized possession of any object or most lounged for relationships, they are to be savoured and enjoyed not just collected on our display shelf. What is the use of having hundreds of connections on our Facebook or LinkedIn, if we don't have time to talk to and help our friend next door?

Hundreds of superficial connects on Facebook
Posts of the places we visit with our new looks
But we don't reach out to friends when needed
Though we have mails, chats, mobile and netbooks.

मुख पुस्तक पर जोड़ रहे हैं रोज नए सतही सम्बन्ध
लुटा रहे हैं अपनी निजता, दिखा रहे अपने आलंभ
पर परिजन के पास पुकारे पर भी नहीं पहुँच वे पाते
यद्यपि सबके पास हुए अब दूरभाष नूतन चलंत ... सशंदु

These are certainly not the exciting times to live if it continues like this..

Have we ever paused and asked this simple question?

What is that we want to achieve to savour the fruits of our life?

In the recent past some of the super achievers died suddenly. While death is something that no one has control over, these events do shake us all. Some reports mentioned about their punishing schedule, tons of tension they carry to achieve super targets quarter after quarter, being hurled on them by senior management. Most of them were rather young, in good physical shape, having no apparent record of any major illness yet they collapsed suddenly on the tread mill, airport lounge or just while boarding their car after a stormy board meeting. There are several other examples where the work related stress has driven people into depression, sometimes in suicide or marital discord. Many early achievers in fashion and film industry get totally disturbed due to initial failures after huge success. Many turn to drinks, drugs and depression leading to suicide in some cases. Just think of the sorrow such actions bring to the parents and well-wishers where you, instead of making them happy, bring additional trauma and pain. It is simply not done—just fight the life, and look for the next day. Other day there was news item that a racing horse collapsed after winning a highly prized race. So what did it achieve at the end, winning the race or dying soon after?

Jeeva also realised that most of these people are no different than him. All of them were neglecting their objectives of larger life and giving importance to material objects alone. The failures to achieve their material objectives were vitiating their entire life. Should it really impact? The extent one should run after the worldly gains and exert himself must be evaluated with respect to one's own abilities. His accident was a just a wake up call for him. He has to find ways to strike a balance between his various objectives of his life.

It was early morning now. The nurse had come to give the morning sponge, but Jeeva signaled her to stop and said, 'Not today. I want to take bath, take me to the bathroom.Help me.'

'Can you?' The nurse asked with a sense of surprise.

'Of course I can. Please lift me up.' He smiled.

When Jeeva put his feet on the ground, it was literally for the first time after his accident. He felt dizzy and then took the support of the bed and sat for a while. He looked at the calendar and realised that it had been 17 days since he came into the critical care unit.

How much day-money do we really have?

These 17days were like many 17 days in his life. But for him they were life defining and ironically life-recharging! Considering an average life expectancy of 75 years for a person, these 75 years have about 27,393 days, 4,38,000 waking hours and 2,19,000 sleeping hours (if taken 8 hours per day). If we spend on an average, 2 hours in commuting, 8 hours of work and 2 hours of personal chores, it leaves only 109500 hours for free use during our life time. After all we just have 3,900 weeks, 900 months in the average life span of 75 years. Whatever it is our life has a limited, finite number!

Most of us think that these life units are endless. We spend our *day-money* thinking that we have them endlessly in our kitty and perhaps can add more of it.[10] In the world where we do not worry about spending because we think we can replenish from the nearest ATM, we extend the same treatment while splurging out days of life on meaningless pursuits. But the life is limited and that too is not certain how much we really have in our kitty. Therefore, every day is important and should be well spent on some meaningful purpose, enjoyment and achievement. Having witnessed that himself when his life was about to end, Jeeva could now see the value of the remaining unknown days!

Key questions we must ask frequently

While going through all these thoughts in his idle body but super active mind, Jeeva ended with the following four questions to prioritise actions for his remaining part of his life. He contemplated theses questions about himself while lying in the hospital bed, many times over as he slowly inched towards recovery.

What does he really expect from his life?

It has been over two decades that he was in a job. There were a number of aspirations, earning money for one and also making a name for himself. But that target always eluded him. Initially it was just any job, then 'that job, that position, etc.' the target continued to move. As he continued to chase sales and project deadline, he lost track of his own personal life targets.

What is the target where he will stop?

Jeeva's career too was like chasing shifting sands. He used to say lightly to his friends that he always got placed in the right department in a wrong organisation. These roles gave him lots of reasons to

[10]Through good upkeep, exercise, yoga, proper care and regular check up and attending to medical issues does prolong the life span.

experiment and fulfill the needs of his creative buds but were low on growth. He was always bestowed with opportunities to do something interesting yet difficult. It was apparent to him that he has not yet defined what he expects out of his own life. Since he has not defined, achieving it was out of question. The attending nurse was very helpful, observing him that he had a penchant for writing and scribbling, she gave him a writing pad. He wrote with his shaking hands on a blank page,

2. What is his career expectations?

A job fulfills several needs for an individual. Besides a source of income, it is also gives occupation, avenues to contribute, opportunities for economic growth and social stature.

- So how much time should one devote to work?
- What type of work?
- Which organisation and for how long?

These questions are tough to answer, partially rooted in the culture and surrounded by which the person belongs to. Indian work culture promotes joining big stable organisation, even if the job content is not too exciting or at times stifling. We see young students, bright and energetic ones, quitting major corporations after few initial years. They say it is not measuring up to their expectations.

So which organisation and which job that one should undertake?

Working for 12 hours a day, 6 days a week is norm in India and many other countries, especially in eastern world. But several researches have proved that the best output one gets from the employees is in the first 40 hours. According to a study[11] published in the European Heart Journal, people spending three or more hours longer at work over and above the stipulated 7 hours a day are 60 per cent more prone to get heart attack or other serious cardiac disease. Another study published by Reuters Life[12] proclaims that those workers who have more flexibility to choose working hours may

[11]http://www.ft.com/cms/s/0/d3526dfa-5d1f-11df-8373-00144feab49a.html (11 May 2010).

[12]http://www.reuters.com/article/idUSTRE61M08I20100223 (22 February 2010).

be healthier in both mind and body than those in less flexible jobs. Slowly increasing set of working population is realising the virtues of flexibility at the work place.

One must at some point in time say 'no thank you' to the culture of overwork and hyper-professionalism. I want to also add another dimension of long and arduous hours that one is subjected to. It is all due to inefficiency of few and unconcern of many that creates this situation. Unnecessary meetings where people walk in unprepared, participate just to make their presence felt, archaic processes that create more work for more people. Parkinson is not wrong when he said that *Work expands so as to fill the time available.*

3. What if... those expectations are not met?

We all run to chase a mirage. That coveted job, that particular role. Those corner room positions or 'A' amount of wealth. But ultimately few will get exactly what they envisaged for themselves. Every now and then when that does not happen, disappointment runs large. The person may hit the proverbial bottle or himself as the case may be. We live in a hyper competitive world where right from the early childhood we are forced to compete almost everyday. Some times to bag a seat in the nursery class and some other times to secure admission in prestigious management college. We feel our life is useless if we are not amongst those bracketed brands.

So what one should do if life does not get as good as one thought? How do we manage the frustrations of our life?

Not everyone will become the movie idol or occupy the corner office. Despite popular award winning movie like *Tare Zamin Pe*,[13] which espoused the virtues of individual excellence, most parameters of a student's success are defined in terms of securing higher marks and grades alone. As a result of which, a child is considered less than ordinary if he is not able to achieve the coveted grades in the exams or secure admission in a school or college of repute. So much is the pressure created by the parents and society that many young minds are not able to cope up with and buckle under. The recent spurt growing suicidal tendencies amongst teenagers is perhaps a direct manifestation

[13]A hit Bollywood movie which lauded the importance of developing special talent of a slow learning child.

of parents (or society) driving them to the brink where they feel there is no way other than to end up their own life!

Failure in jobs too has similar reactions.

Taking risk, trying to do something different invites contempt. Taking career breaks to try out things of one's choice, is a strict no-no. All these are due to our society's inflated expectations to achieve more and more. We have seen people with best of degrees and educations, having a very safe and secured job, yet drive themselves to despair for no rhyme or reason. They perpetually are saddled with *Achievement deficiency syndrome*; because they always want to achieve more. Jeeva too was no different, every stage of his career he felt that he has not got what others have. He always managed to unearth at least one reason to feel dissatisfied whenever he got a promotion, raise or new job with good title or decent salary. He realised during these days, how futile were his expectations and how useless were his carving while gasping for breath and inhaling quality oxygen from the mask.

How much wealth is enough?

Let us say someone defines his sole objective of life to gather wealth and wealth alone. No problem, one can have single point agenda through which the rest of the objectives can be met. A famous ancient verse says, 'Ek sadhe sab sadhe, sab sadhe sab jaye,' which means if you do one thing properly and very well, then all other things will come easily later, but if you start with too many objectives, you end up with nothing.

Yet one need to decide how much wealth is enough and where to stop?

Ironically most of the time our desire to amass wealth is continuously been redefined by looking at what others possess not on what we really need. It is tough to make an escape from the cult of over possession, yet one must decide how much enough to come out of the vicious cycle.

Gautam Buddha says that the wealth does not guarantee happiness and also wealth is impermanent. Take the case of those who chase a superlative goal of amassing wealth. The excessiveness of their 'in satiated desire' for more and more money have driven these super achievers crazy and tempted them to adopt sometimes ingenious yet faulty means. Some of them end up walking in the long corridors of prison or spend significant part of their life battling court cases.

There was no reason for fraudster Bernard Madoff of Wall Street, a former non-executive chairman of the NASDAQ, to go on and on with his money chase while running his ponzi scam. He is believed to have gathered enough wealth to survive many life times, but for his greed remained unabated till he was caught. Now he has lost everything and needs many life times to serve 150 years prison sentence award to him by the courts.

Or back home our poster boy of Indian IT industry from Hyderabad had enough land already that he can ever tile and make mansions on. But he chooses to ride a 'tiger' (in his own words) that he could not get down from. While he betrayed thousands of his well wishers, he himself must be thinking as to why it was necessary for him to do all this when he was to be ultimately declared 'pauper' by an American court.[14]

Some of you may think that these examples are of high and mighty. It rarely applies to lesser mortals like you and me. You may add that if someone gives you just a portion of that kind of wealth and you will stop looking for more. But let me remind you that the greed for more does not only go with people who earn in ten or fifteen digits alone. Just review every day stories on city page of your favorite daily news paper to get the answers. There are crimes like murder, kidnapping or robbery etc., routinely been conducted for few thousand bucks, two room properties, and pocket money to please the girl friend or a new bike by next door people like you and me. They include ever helping neighbors, close friends, good looking strangers and even family members such as son, brother, sister, spouse, daughter, in-laws included. Don't forget the stories of the adulterators, phony chit fund owners, dubious builders and many others who are doing their part of scams irrespective of the value. All these people started small, tasted some success, and wanted to grow exponentially to get rich quickly. Most of them do get caught sooner or later, have horrible family

[14]*The Hindustan Times*, 29th January 2010.

life and live without any respect thereafter. All of them just failed to contain their excessive desire without ever realising that whatever they are striving is really not needed. If any of these criminals would have known where to stop, their life would have turned to better no doubt. Let me assure you that it can happen to any one of us well unless we stop traveling this path of excessive desire which has no destination.

According to the Buddha, teaching true happiness and contentment are possible, if we give up useless cravings and learn to live each day at a time (not dwell in the past or the imagined future). Even if we have been bestowed with excessive wealth through inheritance or having created a successful business, our wealth must be shared with the larger society as many of them started to do or have done in the past. If we adopt this approach our life will become beautiful and enjoyable to live. I don't want to sound idealistic and expect that entire worlds should become saint. All I am saying is that we must know what exactly are our wants and needs, where to put a stop to our useless craving and if destiny has been kind why not share with some of those who are less fortunate and need our support.

Do we all understand what the life gives us?

When Jeeva had a brush with the ultimate truth, (as he used to describe his near fatal accident) he was not sure whether he would be back to normal yet again. Thanks to the efforts of his wife, children, close family members and many of his friends and colleagues he resumed his normal physical chores. Incidentally, a simultaneous transformation that he had in his mental make-up was tremendous and refreshing. While he was a bit slow with his body movement, his mental faculties were working with utmost alacrity and were able to do moreover with complete peace and clarity. Only a person who has undergone such a traumatic experience can find the difference between the value of his life before and after.

Do we really know how one feels when he cannot turn his torso? Even for small tasks he has to press the bell, call the attending nurse even to change his posture. In this condition even taking a short gulp of water needs someone to lift your body with extreme care and hold glass near your lips when you are swallowing[15] just one or two ounces of water. Jeeva never realised that just taking a sip of water was such an arduous task. *One Swallow does not make a summer,* a poetry line Jeeva recalled while he was rested back. But how long will he able to spend his life like this, for how long?

I don't want your imagination to be stretched to visualise some other personal chores, necessary and routine, that we perform at regular intervals. You may laugh, shrug or get embarrassed depending upon which activity comes to your mind. In this condition the patient is dependent on hospital staff or when back home on near and dears to support. Sharing your own very personal space with an unknown attendant or hospital staff is rather tough in these situations.

Many of us would not have gone through this ordeal so it may be a bit hard to imagine. 'But you don't have to! I have lived through that ordeal and learnt on your behalf. I know how helpless one feels when one half of his body goes out of his own control,' Jeeva would say in his opening remarks while conducting *work-life balance*[16] lecture sessions to raptly listening audience later. "It was a time for me to introspect, reflect and resolve to return to life with a vengeance but in a peaceful and balanced manner" he would add. In fact, Jeeva not only wanted to make his life balanced, purposeful and enjoyable but also share the lessons and tips with the rest of the folks who could benefit from it. It is our duty to give back our learning to our fellow life-travellers so that they need not undergo similar hardships to gain the same wisdom.

Returning from the doors of the truth

Death is said to be the ultimate truth. Ironically it comes in only one variety, no matter what form or fashion it may be presented to us. We do get reminded of this very fact when we attend funeral of near and dears and get what is called 'disenchantment at the funeral

[15]Jeeva looked at its dictionary meaning: to take into the stomach by drawing through the throat and esophagus with a voluntary muscular action, as food, drink, or other substances. Well we thought it was easy!

[16]'*Work-life balance* sessions by the author can be conducted free upon request.

pyre.'[17] But these thoughts are soon forgotten as we move on with the glitter of the world and its allure. If death is the ultimate truth we all have to face one day, do we ever think how to conduct and prepare ourselves to face it? Is it worth fighting, biting or hitting each other for worldly possessions that will be left behind any way?

Most of us think that death is something that happens to other people. Yet ask the person who has had experienced a close encounter with it, he will tell an entirely different view of life[18] and death. A person does change his perspective of life when he returns from the doors of the death, if he wants to. The encounter with ultimate truth does make impact to most people.

Our central character Jeeva is like most of our readers. He too was living his life in the fast lane of work, family, investment, achievement. The hours of the day, days of the weeks and weeks of the year would seem passing through like a fast moving train. Ironically this movement was mostly governed by others, imposed by others requirements, punishing schedules and deadlines. Jeeva was living his day as if battling his eyelid, without realising what is going on. In all these years he never ever contemplated the true meaning of his life, what for he has come on this earth. He never pondered with the questions like *why he should live* and *what should he do before he ultimately dies*? He was a confused person, who had no clue how to decide and direct, let alone take control of his life.

But not any more, Jeeva pursued a path to transform his life, even though it happened after a life threatening accident at the peak of his career. Years later, he would thank God for having taught him a wonderful lesson.

[17]This temporary and passing mood of detachment is called *shamshan vairagya* (cremation or burial-ground detachment), or अश्माशन का वैराग्य—a Hindi saying.

[18]The author is not sure if the same sense of dispassion happens to less sensitive people as well. People in the business of close encounter with death, professional warriors, criminals, medical professionals, crematorium staff and many others may adopt a different view, altogether. Even the common people have been found laughing, sharing jokes and doing all that which may not be appropriate while someone's last rights are being performed. Even media folks are blamed to prod people in their grief to get a sound byte and catch sad expressions on their face for few points of TRP!

What is life?

This is rather a baffling question. We all have read the story of Gautam Budhha who was sensitive enough to immensely get disenchanted after watching a dead body, sick and old. He ultimately left his palace, renounced his kingdom to seek the truth of his life. Born and bought up as Siddhatha Gautam, a prince in the foot hills of Himalayas, already a family man with wife and a child, there was no reason for him to get concerned about any of these events that happen all around us every day. Yet he did it and led the world with his new found wisdom.

For Jeeva the story of Gautam Budhha was rather perplexing, though he was greatly impressed by all that The Buddha had to advocate. But leaving the family and kingdom to seek that answer that all of us know, that is, we get old, fall sick and will die one day, was not palatable to Jeeva's consciousness. Armed with all the assortment of new age degrees (engineering, management etc.), having worked with MNCs, Indian mega corporations, having played roles like General Manager, Consultant, Director, President and CEO etc., such thoughts looked amusing and at times foolish to him. Even if they come once in while within the utmost privacy of his own world, he would brush them aside and direct himself to take up pressing work at hand.

Most of us are not insensitive. We do feel pain when someone gets hurt, more so when someone leaves the world. Yet we never think, by pausing a moment to ask a simple question if this is the ultimate truth that we all have to accept one day, what is it that we are preparing ourselves for?

Jeeva recalled a line of Saint Tulsidas,, 'Ab lau nasani ab na lasieho' meaning he has wasted his life so far but not any more. Like Saint Tulsi he decided that he would now devote his life for achieving its larger objectives. So did Jeeva.

Summary of key themes

1. Life is a beautiful present from God that should be lived happily and purposefully.
2. It is finite in nature therefore must be spent meaningfully.
3. A person himself has to take responsibility for his action and inaction of his life.
4. Work and Life are like a pair of feet that need to be balanced.
5. Value whatever you have in possession.
6. Ask 'key' questions to ascertain what your expectations from life are.
7. Take resolve to meet these expectations in a balanced manner.

CHAPTER THREE

Rework YOUR LIFE

> *Success is a process and a combination of things—health, happiness, material prosperity, love of family and friends, wisdom, influence, and fulfillment...... Fred Gratzon*[1]

So, how do we achieve Work Life Balance?

Jeeva was confronted by this question recently. Having luxury of solitude ironically in the hospital recuperating area was forcing him to think about it. He was continuously pondering over objectives of his life, its purpose and how to establish a balance between various dimensions of it. Naturally he had several questions popping up to his mind.

- How can we plan and prepare for work life balance?
- Is there a simple framework that we all can follow to achieve this balance?
- He also desired that any such framework should be easy to remember and apply.

This brought him to the next question as to how can he balance between what he has and what he wanted to have in his life? But he

[1]*The Lazy Way to Success: How to Do Nothing and Accomplish Everything* (Hardcover). by Fred Gratzon.

was not alone or the first person to have this question in this world, he knew very well.

Most of us think about this subject momentarily when confronted with some tragedy or otherwise. Centuries earlier Siddhartha devoted his life finding and defining the meaning of life. Siddhartha concluded in his teachings what one should expect out of this perishable[2] life and how one should live. In fact he left his family and devoted himself entirely to this quest. Siddhartha ended up being a great saint and thinker but in the process he left his wife and children unattended.

Many others who were also driven by similar quest of these life-defining questions, ended up as great saint and visionary but most of them renounced family and worldly goals. Our central character Jeeva was not convinced that 'renunciations' is the only and right way for everyone. If this is so, how will the world and life run? Who will run trains and hospitals, schools and power stations? He was keen to follow grihastha[3] ashram dharma yet achieve what saints have advised. Jeeva was not looking to run away from life but to return to it following a balanced approach.

Budhha's middle path suggest that one should avoid the two extremes *namely* self-indulgence (hedonism) and self-mortification (asceticism).There has to be middle path found for the modern society which neither embraces complete materialism nor complete renunciations. It is the middle path that will lead to vision, to knowledge, to calmness, to awakening and finally to nirvana.

How can we attain nirvana while still being part of the world?

Jeeva's problem solving mind kept on throwing ideas as he was supported by the attending nurse while walking the corridor of the hospital after first few weeks. Doctors had attached infusion pump that was dripping medicine in a controlled fashion directly to his spine. The nurse had brought a stand with wheels to drag the unit along as he has taking mandatory walk in the corridor. It

[2]The Hindi word that captures this property of life is kshan bhangur.
[3]family / home.

was a quite a sight for waiting strangers, who would often stare at him. But he would respond to their stare with wave and smile. Each moment of life from now onwards must bring happiness to others so what if it is the amusing way of his walk that he was learning again, so be it.

Simple framework for work life balance

Jeeva devised a simple framework to address this issue. Conditioned to think in terms of diagrams, charts and 2×2 framework he asked for a paper from the attending nurse and borrowed few coloured pencils from her. She had many pens and pencils tucked in her pocket and gladly gave some to him. She was amused by a sudden bout of activity in the patient. Meanwhile, she grabbed his pulse and pushed a thermometer in his mouth to arrest his enthusiasm. Jeeva continued in his thoughts of three essentials for achieving work life balance.

Essential 1. One must develop a desire to achieve WLB

Jeeva realised that *desire* is the first step of any process to succeed. Last few weeks after reviewing his life, especially what he missed and what he think he should do, had gradually created a strong desire in him to lead a life with happiness, purpose and achievement. He was now convinced that he should strive to lead a well balanced life that addressed all facets not just one, for instance money. He also realised that he himself was at the centre of all his problems, as he had no desire to balance his life. Hence, could not achieve it. Simple!

The work life balance (WLB in short) transformation can only begin with a strong desire from within. For years, Jeeva has read several books and attended many seminars on this subject, and even participated in several research studies to write recommendations about work life balance. But it was nothing different than the story he heard in his childhood about how a flock of birds continued to fall in the trap of bird-catchers, despite being coached by a sage not to fall in their trap. All the birds memorised the holy man's words and continuously chanted, 'Bird catcher will come, put some seeds in and then catch us all in the cage. Let us not fall prey to bird catchers.' Without following its essence they would get finally get trapped. Like many of us who keep on reciting holy names, yet continuously think how to give troubles to others!

Jeeva too was like these ignorant birds, just parroting all the good thoughts but practicing none. But now he decided to act and talk less.

This desire of work life balance can come in each one of us for variety of reasons. One need not wait for life threatening accidents to nudge us to follow good practices. For the rest the desire should come naturally to them before it becomes too late.

Essential 2. We must follow a process, adopt best practices and use appropriate tools

Once a person develops a desire to achieve work life balance he or she should gain knowledge about process or steps, best practice and available tools to walk this path. As a keen stickler for execution, Jeeva knew fairly well that unless these ideas are implemented nothing good will ever happen. Therefore these processes / good ideas must be implemented and their progress tracked meticulously. He developed a simple formats (tracking sheets) to monitor regularly the progress of implementation. (See Chapter 11 for details of various formats.)

All actions will need right implements to facilitate action. The mechanical engineer in him was too keen to look for the right implement to restart the stalled machine called his own 'life'. He knew that tools play a unique part in addressing problem. He was also very fond of emphasising that preparation and planning with the right implements is the key to achieve the objectives faster. He had Abraham Lincoln to help who said *Give me six hours to chop down a tree and I will spend the first four sharpening the axe.*

So he has to follow a suitable process, desired implements and tools to implement what he thought will help in work life balance. The rest of the book (chapter -7 and 9) is all about them, so dear readers please hold on to your curiosity!

Essential 3. Finally the organisation must facilitate a suitable work life balance culture

Finally a fair amount of cooperation and support is needed from the organisation or employers to achieve the work life balance. The organisation must believe that a balance work life is not only needed for the individual but also will help the organisation, ultimately. It must create a suitable environment to facilitate work life balance process.

Work life balance cannot just be achieved by the employees alone. Though individual desire has to be first major step organisation has an important role for the organisation to play. There is elaborate discussion on what an organisation should do is in chapter 8. I suggest those at positions of authority should pick up ideas or two from chapter 8 and implement in their respective organisations. Remember WLB will lead to ultimately benefiting the organisation and thereby the society. It is because its members will lead a balanced life with purpose with lesser tension, and thus produce better results in a cohesive environment. Most employees have realised that facilities like flexibility of the work hours, efficiency of the system and congenial work culture have a strong bearing on the success of an individual. Forward looking companies publicise these aspects as their best practices and convince employees to stay on a long term basis. Lower attrition in an organisation means better results as less energy is wasted on training a new person for the same job.

Chapter 8 details what initiatives organisations should take to help their employees in achieving their work life balance.

Must Develop your own vision for your Work Life Balance

The first step in any journey is the most important one. Having a desire for work life balance is important; the next step is to define a personal vision of the desired work life balance goal.

Like most problem solving situation this was no different for Jeeva. We must start with identification of a vision or goal that we want to

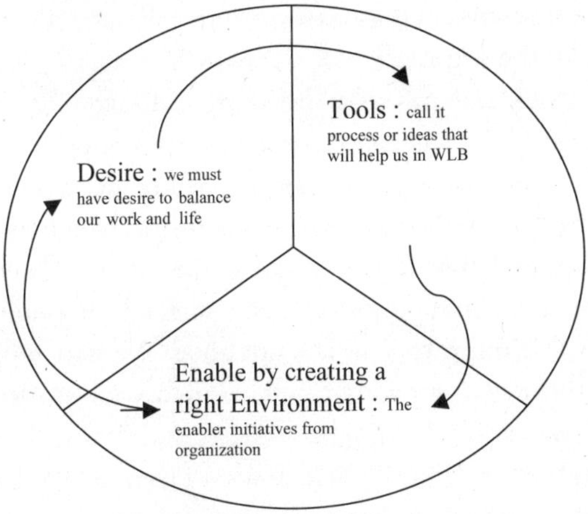

Figure 2. Essentials for WLB: Desire, Tools and Environment

achieve. Having a goal is very important for achieving any thing and he hummed a Hindi couplet that said:

Whoever wanted whatever, achieved it more or less
Those remained contemplating stayed where they were![4]

Most of the time the challenge in our life is to decide what we want out of it! Most decisions are arrived at by looking at others or dictated by others. This process starts when our parents tell us what to do during our initial years. There is nothing wrong to get advice during those formative years as we need someone to guide us. Unfortunately, being always told, to follow or copy others becomes our habit for the rest of our life. As we grow up we start looking at people around us. Be it our friends, teachers, public figures, celebrities etc., who directly or indirectly start influencing us. While this act is absolutely fine till we pick up ideas to firm up our vision. But without a deep understanding about ourselves we will never be able to define our own vision for ourselves. This process of 'being led' continues

[4]जिन्हें जो चाहिय था मिल गया उनको अधिक या कम
हमे क्या चाहिए यह सोचते ही रह गए है हम .... बाल स्वरुप राही

when we start to work in organisation. Our roles and responsibilities are defined by the organisation, mostly by our seniors. Barring few professions where one has some freedom to do what he or she feels like (most creative or entrepreneurial ones fall under this category); in most other professions, the majority of our decisions are taken by people above us in the hierarchy. Sometimes considering them as short term opportunities, we may have made a practical decision and accepted them as a stepping stone. But surrendering our thoughts forever to realise our own vision is not good. We have a firm vision for our life; things that we want to achieve in our life and manoeuvre our efforts towards it.

Now this may look contradictory what I have said so far. On one hand I am advocating to grab the available opportunities yet I am also asking you to create a desired goal of the future for yourself. Let me clarify this a bit.

Just having a vision is not enough. We also have to assess the current situation where we are and then chart out a road map to reach that goal. The desire to reach a destination does not mean that we will always be able to walk 'straight' towards it. The path to our destination may seem to go in the opposite direction, sometimes. As long as we are not wavering in our resolve to head towards the final goal ultimately, we may and sometimes we must, take route that need not point towards the goal exactly. But never loose the focus of your final destination otherwise you end up travelling a road with no destination at all. Honestly, not many of us are fortunate enough to take the shortest or the fastest path in our life, unless we are borne with sliver spoon in our mouth! We always have to negotiate our path towards our desired goal, in a step by step fashion.

Even in the traffic situation on Indian Roads, we seldom get to take the road that is shortest or easiest, because of several restrictions. It may be closed for construction, or may be allowing traffic just one-way. *We sometimes have to drive south in order to reach north,* an anonymous quote Jeeva remembered. This approach is like a constant struggle *between memory and forgetfulness*. Stop the efforts to remember things and forgetfulness will take over your memory.

The next month or so after the accident were too painful for Jeeva. His recovery was slow but steady. The sliver lining of this unfortunate even was that his colleagues, family and friends kept coming back to him to cheer him up. Jeeva realised that he may not have great material wealth to count on but he had greatest wealth of goodwill amongst his near and dear that he could be proud off.

All these people around him were helping him in every manner to get him back to the routine. Before going on medical leave Jeeva used to chair a daily operations Review conference call at 5 pm everyday with his All-India team. He was told that the team was continuing without him regularly with the call and have seamlessly distributed his responsibilities amongst themselves, including the chairing of the call. One day from his hospital bed he decided to join the call when he felt somewhat better. After dialling meeting bridge number, the IVR prompt asked him to state the name and location and he said, 'Jeeva reporting from Apollo Hospital. The confabulation between the participating members immediately stopped in disbelief. After a momentary silence someone asked, 'Who joined?' Jeeva repeated the response. Then there was a huge uproar from the team in the form of 'Jeeva welcome back!'

Jeeva's participation in the initial conference calls were symbolic or at best as a listener. He was not able to speak loudly and for long. Yet it proved his resolve that the show must go on at the work front as well.

Work life balance does not mean to undermine work for life; it means healthy and balanced approach for prosperity and co-existence of both.

But there is a pain that no painkiller can ever alleviate

Back home, with the one arm in a sling and a supporting belt around his chest, movement was restricted within 4 ft by 6 ft of his bed. Jeeva was constantly evaluating the way he was running his life so far. He was contemplating seriously if it is worth living in the fast lane? He remembered several incidents during his life when he just gave precedent to his work and let his personal / family needs be ignored.

He was like hordes of other individuals who consider their career the most important façade of their life.[5]

Today he needed his family and friends to be just around him. No one was solving any of his health related problems. Medicine or time as the best healer were at work, yet he needed them, the way they needed him earlier or will need him sometimes in future. Their just being around was the greatest asset to him, he realised it the hard way. All these events and many more added to his plethora of pains not in the bone or collapsed lungs but deep in his heart that no pain killer will ever alleviate. Yet he knew that the life is not reminiscing about past mistakes or feeling guilty but to take action. The time has come for him to make a new beginning, now.

He decided to do something to bring back the semblance of balance in the remaining part of his life. He was reminded of the story of famous actor Renie who used to play Superman in Hollywood movies. Renie, after a massive fall during a stunt sequence was paralysed neck down. He could hear and understand but cannot do anything using any of his limbs. Despite this he continued to make efforts to live and recover. He even devoted his body for trying out medicinal research for such injuries. He did recover after a lot of clinical trial where he was able to move his fingers a bit before he finally succumbed to his injuries. However, this story shows to us that life irrespective of whatever happens to it is about making suitable and relentless amends for the future.

Value whatever you have in possession

> *Happiness consists not in having what you want, but in wanting what you have..*
>
> —Confucius[6]

[5]According to Hindustan Times Brunch C-fore Survey of Metro cities 58 per cent of the male consider professional success as the most important one for their life. Everything else is secondary. No one wants to be seen as a failure at work. The Hindustan Times Brunch supplement June 27, 2010.

[6]Confucius, 28 September 551 BC–11 April 479 BC. Chinese philosopher whose real name was Kung Fu Tzu or Kung Tzu.

For weeks after the accident Jeeva could not lock the toilet door from inside all by himself. Even if he could lock it, he would fail to unlock it. His right hand had lost its pulling ability and left was in a plaster cast already. He was told that it is the protruding bone on the back called scapula that helps us to pull or push, which was incidentally broken now. He also realised the importance of the left hand, now that it was not available for use. There are certain chores in our daily life with which the left hand is far more adept, efficient and accustomed to deal with than the so-called powerful right hand. We think that left hand is not as useful as the right one but that is not entirely true, a lesson he learnt during this period. This observation also taught him that he should be thankful for whatever he had, good or bad. Every little thing has its own value that we don't cherish. He realised the importance these sentences,[7] which we all must have read many times but seldom take to it to heart and realise its deep significance.

We always try to waste our time and energy to look for something which is not in our possession, not enjoying what we have and valuing it. It is like going to a restaurant and instead of enjoying and savouring our own dish, we look what others have ordered and grump later that we should have ordered that! The other day someone asked Jeeva whether he orders food looking at what others eat in the restaurant or looking at the menu. The answer he gave that he does purely based on his own mind and the menu. In some restaurants where he knows the menu by heart, he just orders irrespective of what others other members of his table are ordering.

In relationships or in our job we always love 'that' we don't have. He remembered a popular story of a blind girl that goes as follows.

[7]*Before you complain about the taste of your food, think of someone who has nothing to eat.*

Before you complain about your husband or wife, think of someone who's crying out to God for a companion. Today, before you complain about life, think of someone who went too early to heaven.—Anonymous. Editor: Please note that I have restyled quoted matter as it would lend better readability.

Story of a Girl:[8] There was a blind girl who hated herself because she was blind. However, she had a loving boyfriend to whom one day she said 'if I could see the world, I will marry you.'

God listened to her plight and one day someone donated a pair of eyes to her. When the bandages came off, she was able to see everything, including her boyfriend.

He asked her, 'Now that you can see the world, will you marry me?' The girl looked at her boyfriend, but alas that he too was blind like her. This discovery took her by surprise.

Now that she had a pair of beautiful eyes she had become wiser. The boy friend that was around for so many years was less than desirable with his empty eye-cups. So with all her newfound wisdom, she refused to marry and settled with someone else.

After some time she received a note from her ex-boyfriend, which read, 'Take good care of your eyes, my dear, for before they were yours, they were mine.'

We can see the world, therefore, we want more! The new-found vision of the girl made her abandon a choice that was so dear to her few weeks back during her dark days.

I am neither against moving on with life nor in favour of clinging on to the past. But at any time we should consider twice before dumping the past that was so useful, be it an object, a relationship or a memory. One should have the conviction and courage to seamlessly maintain the linkages with the past as one forges new ones with the future. Like old wine, relationships taste better over time. Here are few lines with which I end this chapter.

There's one sad truth in life I've found
While journeying east and west—
The only folks we really wound

[8]Source: Anonymous.

Are those we love the best.
We flatter those we scarcely know,
We please the fleeting guest,
And deal full many a thoughtless blow
To those who love us best.

—Ella Wheeler Wilcox[9]

Summary of Key Themes

Follow a simple Desire, Tools, Enabling environment (DTE)work life framework to prepare yourself. The DTE framework comprises of:

1. Desire to have a work life balance: Start with desire and develop your own vision for your work life balance.
2. Know and use necessary tools to achieve it: theses are processes or ideas that will help us in WLB.
3. Work in or create an environment within your work organisation to facilitates work life balance: These include enablers and facilities from the work-organisation that will help in work life balance.
4. Value what ever you have in possession.

[9]Ella Wheeler Wilcox (American poet and writer 1850-1919).

CHAPTER FOUR

Take ACTION

> *Good thoughts are no better than good dreams, unless they be executed!*
>
> *—Ralph Waldo Emerson (1803–1882)*

Five simple steps for work life balance

Jeeva was getting back to the path of physical recovery. He felt that at least he should complete the thinking and planning part of his WLB efforts. While following the doctor's advice and prescription for physiotherapy and his medicines were helping his body, he needed to draft an agenda for his overall balanced recovery for the rest of his life.

The first and foremost step in any problem solving is to assess the current situation. Is his life really unbalanced or it is just a myth? By asking several introspective questions[1] he came to a conclusion that his life indeed was not in a balanced state. It was too slanted towards his career and work requirements, on earning material wealth and emulating the rest of the world in a perpetual rat race. Moreover, he was also confused as to whether he was travelling the right path in his life.

[1]Refer Chapter 11 A. WLB quiz: Test how balanced you are?

He needed to ask some simple questions to identify the right approach that will bring back necessary balance in his life. He continued with his thought process to come up with the following five steps to continue his exploratory journey on WLB path after reading several books and researching this subject on the internet:

1. *Define what he wants to achieve realistically in his life*: Call it a vision or goal that each one us must define and assess from time to time. Living a life without a goal or what one really wants is travelling a road without a destination in mind. He reads books, literatures, scriptures and ancient stories extensively to arrive at his own goals in life.
2. *Assess the extent to which his current role/job is meeting his needs:* Arriving at the vision was seemingly tough but the current assessment proved to be tougher. He for one found that most of his goals were too far away from what his current role, job or state of the life. It was as if he was travelling towards down south looking to climb the Himalayas!

   To his surprise, he was not alone in his struggle. At different occasions when he broached this subject with his colleagues or friends, they had similar confusion. All of them were shying away from this discussion and postponing it for some other day. Fortunately, the confinement had given him the opportunity to confront this question repeatedly and find a way that would change his perspective of life for the better, and forever.

   Why this confusion about goals of life, where we are and what to do? It is simply because we never pause to think where we want to go, what have we achieved already and when we think we can feel satisfied? But you are having this question then there is nothing to be alarmed with. You are not alone in this quest. There are very few people who could do or are doing what they wanted to; all others have to struggle to get back to their desired state, the way Jeeva did.

   Jeeva looked at his current job and first focussed on its positives. Most of the time we quickly identify the negatives of any job. Perhaps our analytical and critical mind is conditioned to finding faults with everything. In his life too every change that he undertook in the past, he quickly found out its negatives and stared whining and cribbing. But not any more.

The other day my friend Prakash called me to share the news about his new job in a very reputed company. He was struggling to find one for several months. When I said how he feels, his first response was that the office is too far off! He just forgot to talk about the positives and only identified the negatives so far. Ask anyone how is life and the reply will vary from 'not too bad' to 'just ok' to 'lot of problems' and you can make who is focusing on positives and who is only worried about the negatives.

Once Jeeva was able to identify the positives of his profession/job he felt so comfortable that he felt like taking a walk on his own. He balanced his body in such a way that he was able to get up without the aid of anyone. He quietly got up but felt a bout of dizziness. He leaned at the corner of the bed. The nurse came running to assist him but he waved her to let him manage himself. Finally he could stand of his own and slowly walk, unassisted. This was a good metaphor for him where he on his own decided to change the current situation (lying on the bed) to the next step of standing of his own, before his desired situation of moving quickly and swiftly.

But he could do all this only when he decided to act on his own!

3. *Prioritise key areas for action:* We want so many things in our life and interestingly, all of them now! Such ambitions are too hard to realise for most of us. We need to prioritise our needs depending upon different stages of our life, even at different parts of the year, month and day. Remember we can never have everything all together.

For instance during the kids vacation time, he decided to prioritise his work such that he could be with them for longer and also take a week or two off to travel with them, something that he never did in the past. Earlier, he was supposedly the most useful and valuable guy in the office during school vacation time who would not take leave during school holidays. Once he did go to his boss asking for leave because he had plenty of them unutilised. His boss instead of allowing him to proceed on leave gave him a sermon for the next 15 minutes to convince him that a person of his calibre must not take leaves just because it is likely to lapse. Instead he should continue to attend pressing issues at work. However, the very next day his boss himself disappeared to consume his own lapsable leave to manage his own work life! Jeeva realised that only he was to be blamed for not planning his leave well in advance and let it remain unutilised till it became lapsable.

At different stages of life, our priorities have to be different. Ancient Indian scriptures talk about five stages of life. Starting with childhood, life moves on through years of youth, family life, retired life and finally living a life of a recluse. In fact, during the last two stages of the life one is supposed to start 'to withdraw' from worldly attachments' and devote time in intensely prayer-oriented routine.[2] Jeeva too needed to prioritise key areas for his current stage of his life.

4. *Draft a plan of action*: Once you have defined where you want to reach, deliberated on your priorities and also assessed your current situation, it is time to take actions.

Jeeva defined that one of the priority of his life to take care of the children's education at that stage of his life. The last few months of his confinement has given his children extra maturity and a sense of responsibility. For Jeeva, the first priority was to resume normal day to day chores of his own as soon as possible. He meticulously followed doctor's advice to gain strength and self-confidence. In addition he picked up the threads of his work responsibility slowly. He started answering mails from his home, joining conference calls for key meetings and mentoring the team as well. But now he would ensure that he be released from meetings or conference calls to attend his physiotherapy sessions as well. The colleagues and customer were too keen to support. He realised that it was he who did not demand or request in the past for such accommodation to take care of his personal life. Something that was available for asking in progressive organisations like his own that is willing to extend such flexibility to its employees.

Amongst other priorities were his finances, taking care of his hobbies and of course social and other responsibilities. He revived his hobby of writing while lying in bed using his laptop. Several manuscripts, half written for over decades were discovered from

[2]more about it in Chapter 5.

dusty cabinets. Earlier he had nothing interesting to look up to when he was at home or during the weekends. Consequently he was chasing more work to fill his evenings and weekends. This change helped him rekindle some other targets in his life. He recalled that in the past he would be so engrossed in his work responsibilities that he would spend his entire weekends doing just the office work. All these have to stop. He decided not to force schedule late evening meetings to push his team and himself. His team naturally felt good when they came to know of this change. He started devoting extra quality time with his wife and family and they now had fewer complaints to make.

5. *Take action and be happy with whatever you have!*
   The most important part of this frame work is to take relentless action not only to bring work life balance but also be happy with whatever one has. In the internet age where the happiness is defined by material possessions alone and prestige through job title, being just plain happy within your means has been totally forgotten. Having aspirations is understandable but if you are perpetually chasing mirage after mirage, it will exhaust you.

साईं इतना दीजिये जा में कुटुंब समाय
मैं भी भूखा ना रहूँ साधू न भूखा जाय
रूखा सूखा खाई के ठंडा पानी पीव
देख बिरानी चूपरी मत ललचाना जीव[3] ....रहीम

Never make your aspirations propelled by looking at other's achievements. Even if you want to raise the bar, follow your own self as a standard. This realisation was very useful to Jeeva and he stopped feeling unhappy looking at other's achievement and felt just happy with himself, his achievements and also his limitations.

He recalled a Persian proverb:

I scowled because I had no shoes on my feet, until further down the street I saw a man with no feet at all.

[3]God Give me as much so that I can feed my family, neither I should remain hungry nor the visiting guest eat simple meal and drink cold water, never look at others buttered bread and hanker for it.

How do we balance the portfolio of our life?

Portfolio approach is widely used for managing personal investments and projects for businesses. Taking a leaf from the same, we need to create a balanced the portfolio of our life. When we understand the major heads that constitute a balance portfolio of life, only then we can embark to travel a path of work life balance.

Ancient Indian wisdom envisages that our life rests on the following four pillars:

- Artha (money)
- Dharma/Karma (duty)
- Kama (enjoyment, sensual pleasure)
- Moksha (leaving a legacy of good deeds to attain salvation)

Like in financial planning where we need to have a mix of investment based on our age, risk appetite, responsibilities etc., we have to put different priorities on these four areas of life-investments. Since our time and effort will always be limited we need to keep changing the effort-mix as we progress in our life's journey. Our goal in life also has to keep changing based on the stage we are at and what can be achieved with available options and abilities.

Let us take out a pen and a paper to develop the goals for each of these pillars of life.

- **Artha** (money): What should be our source of income and how much income is enough for a reasonable living? Remember for most of us enough is never enough. One must be careful to arrive at a realistic goal which he/she is capable of achieving it in reasonable time frame. Not only are we created and groomed differently, our abilities and skills are also different. We also must accept that results may not always come in a direct proportion to efforts and there is a factor of luck and otherwise. Therefore, one should define the Artha goal with caution and with an assumption that acquiring wealth through honest means will always be slow and difficult.
- **Dharma** (duty/responsibility): This defines the roles or responsibilities that we have to undertake for the self, family or our professional life. The word *Dharma* does not represent our religious inclination but covers what are our rightful acts and deeds that we should do while adhering to certain principles.

Sage Manu in his ancient text *Manusmriti* recommends 10 essential rules to follow while discharging our duty (dharma) for self, family or professional life.

- Have Patience (dhriti),
- Allow Forgiveness (kshama),
- Have Piety or self-control (dama),
- Follow Honesty (asteya),
- Attempt Sanctity (shauch),
- Attempt Control of senses (indraiya-nigrah),
- Follow the Reason (dhi),
- Strive for Knowledge or learning (vidya),
- Be truthful (Satya), and
- Manage / mitigate anger (krodha)

Following these principles in day to day life makes us more controlled and calm. Our professional activities should also be guided by these principles as described above.

- **Kama** (enjoyment): How much worldly pleasure to seek? This goal is related to our pleasure coefficients that can come through emotional relationship and sensual pleasure, eating, travelling and enjoying fruits of the nature and man made wonders. Kama in other words also represents the basic philosophy on which the human origin is based. Indian culture respects its necessity and spirituality associated with this. Yet its also teaches us to abhor its excesses.

A well balanced life is largely a manifestation of a well achieved emotional balance. Domestic happiness and enjoyment cannot be achieved just by earning a lot of wealth or doing your duty as prescribed in the scriptures. Had this been the case, a number of high profile celebrities would not have had atrocious relationships in their life. They were driven by the enjoyment factor alone and then ended up disenchanted despite their wealth or professional achievements. I am neither labelling Kama as being either unnecessary or negative. Kama has its own due importance in our life. Without enjoyment life will be too staid and uneventful to live. God has created this wonderful world for us to enjoy our life. We have every right to relish what it offers and what we can afford. The world progresses because human beings want a better life, enjoy and derive pleasure from it.

Yet, we must observe moderation while enjoying the fruits of the world.

- **Moksha** (salvation): 'Mokshya' or 'moksha' or 'mukti' is a Sanskrit word that stands for 'liberation'. The traditional meaning of this word is to show how a person can achieve liberation from the incessant cycle of death, birth and reincarnation and ultimately find salvation. Jeeva's scientific mind reinterpreted this word as liberation from worldly traits.

  How can a person raise his or her level of intellect through spiritual activity so that he (she) becomes 'Sthitpragya'? A state the *Bhagwad Gita* defines for a personality who has a steadfast intellect and unwavering mind that does not show aggression, hostility, anxiety, hatred and anger. Once a person reaches that stage he travels to the path of salvation. Mokshya also covers the legacy that we want to leave behind for the larger goods of the world behind. Our birth on the earth is not just to enjoy, plunder and then go away but also to do something so that the world sustains the way our predecessors have done to us through their contribution.

Jeeva also realised that all these four pillars of his life need to be properly balanced. Without going too much into the theory, he decided to create a simple work sheet for goals he would pursue for next 3–5 years for each of these four pillars of life.

(Readers may fill one for themselves using template B in Chapter 11)

He noticed that filling up these columns were not easy. In some cases he was not sure what all to include or what to exclude from the list of his goals (Column 1, 3). In some cases he was at a loss as to what should his goals be, as everything seems to be a routine and insignificant.

Distinguish between Wants and Needs: We must be careful to focus on what is our real need and what are our wants. We should not just fill the columns with all our wants.

Everyone needs financial Independence. We need enough finance to be free to pursue our dreams. We will need a source of income

TABLE 4.1 Jeeva's Balanced Goals for Next 5 Years

	Artha	Karma /Dharma	Kama	Mokshya
Define your Goal	Build a kitty of $$$$$	1. Complete current project successfully 2. Discharge Family Responsibilities	World tour with family Own luxuries as per a list discussed with Family	Being seen as person without any greed, grudge or excessive desire. Mentor and give back knowledge to those who need
Define Your current state	1/5 th of the Goal	1. Project at a critical stage. 2. Children currently in School	Some of them obtained	Many areas need to work
Prioritise key areas	Fresh investment Stability of income **Priority** 1	1. Adequate recources for the project 2. 2. Children Education grooming to face the real life **Priority** 2	First he will undertake short tours, when he becomes better he will drive distances and then long after 3 years he will take an overseas tour **Priority** 3	Give back knowledge Spiritual learning **Priority** 4
Draft a plan of action	Wiser investment, Stop Speculation, Adequate Insurance cover,etc.	Spend more time every week with the family	• Undertake at least one holiday in next 5 months • Undertake one religious tour to thank God for saving his life before year end	Package knowledge into accessible form for wider audience. Spread spirituality amongst friend

that helps us to sustain a reasonable living. We also some times need to splurge, travel places and enjoy other worldly pleasures. For all this financial independence is a must. Yet one needs to decide how much money is enough and where do we put a cap on our standards of living.

You also may start to note down your important needs in the template and work towards achieving them while I tell you more about Jeeva quest for work life balance.

Jeeva contemplated his financial independence by focusing on his simple and basic needs. He ascertained that he must have his own house to live by the time he attains certain age. He must also have a regular source of income post his retirement. In earlier days our ancestors used to have agricultural land, fruit orchards or just house property that could fetch rent as a regular income. An old vernacular saying of an Urdu poet, Ghagh came to his help

उत्तम खेती माध्यम बाण अधम चाकरी भीख निदान[4]

He looked at his current living standards and decided a target income that he needs every month to suffice his kitchen and house hold expenses. In addition, he planned for other expenditures and arrived at target kitty at an age of his retirement. Any financial planner would help in deciding this goal based on inflation index, etc. He took help of few of them and based on their advice distributed his investment into safe investments, some in equity, paid off the unnecessary loans of house, car, furniture etc., and made himself *debt free*. He also made a habit of reviewing his personal balance sheet periodically and decided that he would be cautious and prudent with his investment as he is with his expenditure.

After his planning for the first pillar of life Artha was done he felt a lot comfortable.

Dharma, duty, engagement, sense of achievements (his day to day Karma): Having just money in your pocket is not enough. A person is known for the kind of job he does or responsibility he or she

[4]Uttam Kheti, madhyam baan; adham chaakri bheek nidaanan translated it means that best profession in the world is production (call it agriculture, village artisans and all modern form of hard or soft products creation will fall under this category),the second best being trade where you serve others who produce to sell their goods. The lowest option is service and begging is the worst of all.

carries (or have carried in the past). It is important for all of us to have a reasonable rise in the status that we can claim as our achievement. One must have a goal to achieve in this, even though he may have inherited enough from his parents and ancestors.

Few lines of the famous Hindi poet Maithali Sharan Gupt are very apt to encapsulate these thoughts.

Kuch kaam karo, Kuch kaam karo, Jag mein rah kar kuch naam karo
Yeh janma hua kis arth aho, Samjho jismein yeh vyartha na ho.
Sambhlo ki suyog naa jaye chala, Kab vyartha hua sadupaay bhala
Akhileshwar hai avlamban ko, Nar ho naa nirash karo man ko[5]

The theory of Karma underlines that all individuals are responsible for their past and present actions. We are judged by what we do and how we do. Our status in the society is directly proportional to the office or position we achieve in our life. This is a fact and we must strive to reach certain level in our career. Yet the sense of achievement may not just come from the hierarchical levels alone that we attain. Status acquired only due to hierarchy of office is always transient in nature. This status goes away the moment that position is lost. You may retire, get retrenched or resign depending up on the situation. In that respect a social service, creative work also gives an everlasting respect. The fact is that any achievement would give you a respect; it may not only come from your job or profession alone but also from other acts of service or contribution that you make in the society.

There was a mill foreman named Mishra *ji* who had enormous respect in the community for his alternate practice of Indian medicines. His job had nothing to do with his outside philanthropic activities. Not only was this activity a small source of added income but a huge respect for him within the community. Similarly, Jeeva recalled Jain *Sahib* whose day job was behind the counter in a library but had also developed a huge clientele of life insurance policy holders who

[5]Translated it means, you must do something to get name and fame as you have be destined do something to make worth of your life. Get your acts together before the opportune time goes away and your effors will never go in vein. God always helps those act and never get disheartened. by famous Hindi Poet Shri Maithilisharan Gupt (1886–1965).

used to look upto him for various occasional help and advice that he was most willing to give.

A well-known professional from the world of advertising is also known for his poetic prowess and who has penned several chart buster songs for Hindi movies. A chief justice form a state high court is also a well known authority on astrological predictions. In addition there are several week-end theater personalities and writers who churn out stellar stage performance or best selling fictions to add to their list of achievements. This is not to say that only secondary or creative achievements are worth noting. Visionary people like Verghese Kurien, who is known as the Father of White Revolution in India (dairy), Jamshed ji Tata who laid foundation of Tata group of companies a hundred years ago, noted environmentalist philosopher and activist Sundarlal Bahuguna who led Chipko movement against the felling of trees in Himalayan states, are examples where their achievements were not because they held any position but what they achieved as their life time ambition.

So whether it is the achievement within the stricter sense of profession, alternate creativity or social service, one must decide a goal, achieve them while still maintaining balance with his/her life. Many people develop alternate career or useful hobbies to ultimately take is as post retirement option. This also keeps them somewhat insulated form the ups and down of the job cycle, not just monetarily but emotionally.

It is not un-natural when someone meets with accident of a serious nature, his or her confidence gets shaken up and desire to live gets somewhat diminished. However, it is the sense of responsibility that propels him to recover from the ashes to overcome his physical disability. It was late in the afternoon when Jeeva desired to drink water but was unable to get up on his own. The nurse was also not around nor could he grab the bell normally kept close to his reach. He thought he must overcome this handicap and dialed a friend's number who was waiting in the reception area. The friend in turn called up the hospital staff to reach out to him. This simple step reassured him that technology is great assistance in managing life in the modern days and he must explore it as much as possible.

While Jeeva was contemplating his goals for his life, he also looked around to assess his unfinished tasks. Thanks to the words of his friend

Aditya who reminded him not to loose heart or get discouraged by his temporary set back. 'As a bread earner of the family you must get well soon to discharge your responsibilities', he added. Another colleague Ravi was more forthright narrating his personal experiences and nudged him to return to life as fast as possible. 'Do not get concerned just because few of your limbs were not working at 100 per cent efficiency. Why not start coming to the office just for few hours and after some time gradually increase the duration as you feel better,' he advised. Even the attending doctors advised him to take on as much work as he can but without getting too tired.

Develop a sense of security to feel comfortable: We all need security it in various forms or fashion. When we were children we used to hide in the laps of our mothers/ grandmothers whenever we felt afraid of darkness or ugly creatures. We all continue to behave the same way and look for places to hide, despite growing up. We settle in a community where we have people with similar origin, spoken language, country or state. In terms of a job we look up to a stable job, a well-known brand and an organisation that provide us a sense of security. The need for security and its desire is inherent in the human psyche.

If we plan for building securities early enough in our life, better would be our judgement while devoting time to our profession at later days. Call it financial, social or emotional security, we must try to provide for it sooner than later. There are certain careers that are like 'shifting sands' which have lots of uncertainty and changes very frequently. Some others have short span, examples of which are sports, fashion or media. Some have a lot of gestation to prosper or reach a stable level, politics and medical profession fall under this category. And finally there are careers that seem to take off only for one amongst a hundred thousand; being a writer is one example! In all these chameleon careers, camphor-like career or career of building castle in the air requires an alternate support system to give you a sense of security. The great Olympian shooter Abhinav Bindra from India could build his career because the family was willing to invest in his training and support which an ordinary person would have found difficult to do. So is the career of several second generation film stars who are launched with hype by their parents. For the remaining ones, who make their career generation after generation afresh, the approach of creating a secured base is important for financial, emotional and social level. A well thought out plan of security will also help us set limits to our risk taking abilities and choosing career, profession or jobs with care.

Trigger of change

When the body started to regain its strength, mind its confidence, and soul its new found wisdom, Jeeva felt like someone who is expectant to usher a change and embrace a new life. He knew pretty well that nothing will happen overnight. His habits, work routine, pattern of expectations or lack of it that he had created within his work place or with his family by being his workaholic self, would not be erased easily. He has to take several steps demonstratively and relentlessly over time to come out of his legacy.

Fortunately his family, friends, colleagues and even his organisation was too willing to support. He was indeed a lucky man because he had so many good people around him. He was amazed to see so many good people belong to his community. He was overwhelmed by their advice, help and support. Be it the get-well-soon mails, cards and flowers sent by his friends from all over the country and abroad or just a casual 'hello' by those who dropped by his bed side for few minutes. When the limit of the medical insurance was reached while he was still in the hospital, his colleagues made extra efforts to seek necessary approvals from the office administration to carry out the treatment uninterrupted. He cannot forget the personal attention he received from family, friends and colleagues who stood by him during the tough time and gave him support.

He decided to take few baby steps. The past cannot be corrected but the future can be.

Manage your day efficiently and effectively

Like the packet of energy described in quantum physics, day is the most valuable unit of our life. One must manage the day efficiently, effectively and in a balance way. We should avoid erratic work schedules, day stretching to wee hours either for study, work or party are all enemy of balanced and healthy living.

Most people struggle with their daily routine. Unless you are able to manage your day well, how well will you manage your week, month, year or your entire life? The other day a person was contemplating a job between salaries of ₹90,000 against ₹65,000 per month. The only difference was that the first one had a commute time of 2 hours either way. What do you think the person would have chosen and what do you think you would chose in such situation?

Meticulously plan and be efficient: All our days come in just one size of 24 hours. This is one size that is available to all: be it the Prime Minister or a common citizen, everyone has to fit his activities within these hours only. For Jeeva managing his day well was the first action to accomplish. Planning the day in advance and reviewing whether it was well spent at the end of the day was a good habit he found useful. With series of meetings and several client visits seeking his attention, now he would visualise when will he do what? Getting up a little early by 5:30 am was proving to be very useful. Incidentally this routine was also introduced to him in the hospital by the night shift nursing staff who had to prepare the patient after they finished their morning chores. So that these patients are ready in time for Doctor's early morning round. When he rejoined his work, his starting early meant less traffic on the road, less fuel consumption and lots of peace of his mind.

He became more efficient in running meetings. He would stop colleagues from unnecessary conversations in the meetings and also keep a tab on his 'to-do' list meticulously as the day progressed. He found that his email turn-around improved dramatically and his sense of having done a fair share of work every day increased significantly.

Must say no to work assignments sometimes: He was one such person who would never say no to any work assigned to him whatever may be the deadline. He was always considered a hard working guy, dedicated and loyal to his work. He was rewarded with six promotions in as many years. But all that was in lieu of the sacrifice he made on the part of his family time. He realised that he should have said no to such work, given to him either because someone else was slow, slack or unwilling. He either acted too meek to protest the loss of family time or took pride in being fooled. Taking extra initiative is fine but it should not lead to compromising his freedom of devoting time for himself or to his family.

Be assertive and delegate often: He decided to be assertive to say no if it is too much for him to take. He took a short course of assertiveness and consulted few books on delegation and learnt the art of 'push back'. He would not accept task that he was not supposed to do. Also he won't worry that everything should be finished in the same day by him.

Must say no to excessive social engagements: He decided to regret attending networking dinners after business meetings. He would apologise to the host as soon as the drinks will be served to leave the venue early so as to reach home in time of dinner with the family. As a teetotaller he had no fancy for hard liquor and therefore no inclination to waste hours on unnecessary gossips over drinks. He had to balance himself carefully between the two extremes, one being dubbed as unsocial and the other being a party animal that party's hard till wee hours!

In order to manage the work-task he has to do, he arrived at a simple model for managing his daily routine efficiently and effectively. Unless he becomes efficient and effective in work he can not find time for his family and for himself

He gave a name to this simple model as **FLIP Model as shown in figure 4.1**.

Finish always what you take up, don't start anything unless you want to finish. Life is too precious to waste on half done jobs.

- *Prioritise* what needs to be done every hour, everyday and every week. The good old school class time table has its merits and must be used to schedule the day. For example, there are certain times in the day when it is easier to plan, some other for meetings and some for brain storming or follow up. It all depends on personal preferences but the morning hours are considered better for planning and afternoon for meetings and follow ups. Similarly, you should decide the days of the week which you will devote for

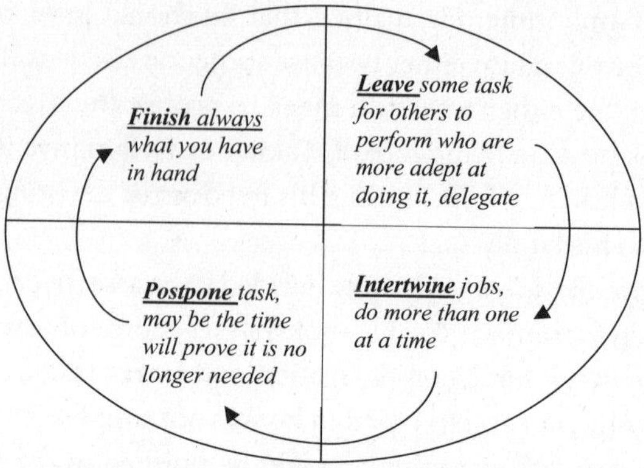

Figure 4.1 FLIP Model

certain types of work. Remember, you have to manage your time efficiently despite the pressure from others.

- *Break* every job into small tasks, so that you can complete each one of them in two or three sittings. Always stop at logical break points so that it is easier to resume thereafter.
- *Do* the easiest job first. It will act as an incentive to you as your completed list will swell early in relation to the uncompleted task list.
- *Set a schedule* to complete all jobs, otherwise they can linger forever. If you have completed any task early, reward yourself. Take a stroll, look around, talk to folks or just listen to music on your cell phone. After all you deserve a break often.

Leave some tasks for others to perform who can do it better and faster, far more efficiently and professionally. You need to know the art of delegation and finding people who are capable, available and amenable to do such job. They must also fall under the sphere of your influence. You should be able to tap their capabilities and time to make use of them, at a cost that you should be willing to undertake. Remember any thing that saves your time is worth considering.

In order to delegate your task better you should:

- Specify exactly what you want to accomplish. Be considerate of the risk of non-completion or loss of quality when delegating the first time.

- Delegate with good description, dos and don'ts. Also make sure that the instructions are properly understood by the person who will carry out the task.
- Set a schedule for the completion, check the progress often but not too often.
- Avoid micromanagement; give room to the doer to explore. Coach him / her on the objectives and share some tips of the job, but let him / her do the job.
- Be tolerant if the task is not completed exactly the way you specified, it will surely improve over time

***Intertwine jobs*:** Technology gadgets, if used properly can help us intertwine more than one task to add variety and also accomplish them in parallel. Use of microwave oven in cooking is one example where you don't have to watch the dishes being cooked if you know the parameters at which the oven is to set. It is possible to reply to the emails while listening to music or do some transactions like approving leave or travel bills. Conference calls take a big chunk of the executive time these days; some mundane task can be performed during this period. Jeeva developed routine to make personal calls while being driven to or back from the office. He would answer his emails from within the confines of his car without being stressed to watch the slow movement of traffic. He recalled his wife doing exactly the same when she continues to fold laundry, cut vegetable and also watch TV at the same time.

Two for one can be fun!

***Postpone tasks*:** This is good one if you understand the essence of this thought well. This thought is not to advocate procrastination or adding lethargy to your work but something else. Many tasks don't need immediate attention, they can wait till they become pressing for action. Many other tasks are supposed to be done only after a reasonable time of wait. For example, you need not rush to deposit a cheque as soon as a utility or credit card bill arrives. All mail coming over a weekend should wait till the weekend is over unless it is from your boss asking for a piece of information for his board meeting on Monday morning at 9 am.

A former prime minister of India has supposedly once said 'not taking a decision some times is also a decision'. Family Court some times does it very well in marital dispute cases. It does not take up all the cases as soon as they are filed but gives next date of hearing. In some cases it reserves a decision till next week or two to allow intervening time to gather more facts or better sense between the warring parties.

Let us not think that everything has to be done today and now. If the job does not need to be done immediately, leave it for another time. One need not reply to a mail as soon as it lands in his / her mail box or the start thumbing as soon as an SMS comes in mobile message box. We must allow emails and SMSs some time to 'brew' in their respective in-boxes before we act on them. You will find that in many cases problem itself will disappear in few hours. There is no point being 'mail-happy' to answer a mail as one is called 'trigger happy' when he shoots aimlessly just because he has a gun in his hand.

Postponing and procrastination are different. The case of the former, one deliberately decides to do the task at another appropriate time and that too when the time is right. The later is an act of indecision which is purely a result of lack of desire and must be avoided at any cost.

This was one of the useful mantra for work life balance which helped Jeeva in setting expectations with his friends and colleagues in the long run.

Simplify life

'Our lives are frittered away by detail; simplify, simplify.'

—Henry David Thoreau (1817–1862)

Our modern day life has become very complex with umpteen demands on our time from variety of activities around us. The onslaught of technology has put in more complications in our lives. Each gadget clamors for more attention and more time from us. With two mobile phones, Blackberry and of course our age old land line, one can perpetually be talking to someone or the other throughout the day. When do we get free time to think and talk to ourselves?

Then there are half a dozen email accounts to be looked at, networking sites, fun sites to visit, which can take few hours easily just to clear spam mails, attachments carrying funny jokes, self-help presentations or peppy jpg files. Then occasionally you get forwarded mails that demand that you must forward it immediately to 20 others to get divine blessings, however, if you ignore the request you could be doomed!

All these time wasters should be avoided.

How easy it was in the olden days when there were no phones or emails. There was no interruption from telemarketers or favour seekers. Life was simple.

Reduce Transaction overload: Jeeva decided to take few steps to simplify his life. He surrenders several credit cards and loyalty programme cards that were occupying his wallet unnecessarily. Numerous discount vouchers and promotional offers that land in our mail box create more confusion and feeling of guilt if we don't use them. He decided to curtail their usages, and also reduced the number of his on-line accounts. He needed only a few for his regular uses. At least he will not waste his time either reading their statements, filing them for Income tax purposes or writing multiple cheques month after month. He also decided to do away with all his dormant bank accounts and non-performing shares. Finally he developed work life balance sheet[6] to calculate how much time he was wasting on unnecessary tasks daily and continued to monitor his progress month after month thereafter

Speak truth: Lao-tzu (604 BC–531 BC) author in his book *The Way of Lao-tzu* gives some plain advice to simplify our lives. He says 'Manifest plainness, Embrace simplicity, Reduce selfishness and have few desires'. Simplicity is the biggest effort one can make to strike a work life balance. Simple things like speaking the truth ensures that you don't remember what lies you have told and to whom!

Have few but solid relationships: Every relationship has its own attention overload to manage them. There is no need to have 500+ connections on a social networking site if we don't have time to

[6]Refer Chapter 11. Annexure J. Draw your work life balance sheet to arrive at an assessement of how your life is simple or complex.

nurse few solid relations. Most such sites add mass mails by attention grabber's members for their self-promotion and self-publication. Jeeva decided that he would not let his time become a fodder of the idling pursuit of such individuals. He removed himself from many networking sites; several online groups to free up more time for his few solid relationships.

Such steps do not mean we should become recluse or aloof from rest of the world. Having a mile long list of friends assembled over the years will have its own overhead on our limited time. Just think of the transactions in case your mail id and mobile number reaches to exponentially growing list of marketers through such 'free-sites'. The daily routine will have unnecessary distractions for no apparent benefit.

Remove noise: To simplify our lives we will have to remove the unnecessary noise form our surroundings. It is not essential to watch all programmes from all entertainment channels and track all the T20 matches that are going on somewhere. Try switching off TV one of these days and you will be surprised that you have recovered so much of your quality time.

To quote Thoreau once again 'most of the luxuries and many of the so-called comforts of life are not only not indispensable, but positive hindrances to the elevation of self'. Jeeva recalled how much care free his days were when he had few clothes to fill his modest almirah. Those days he also had not so many vehicles to look after. The problem of plenty has put in more demand on his time to look after his cars and other objects of his interest for their upkeep, servicing, insurance maintenance etc.

Use technology judiciously: (unplug few unnecessary gadgets) Computer, a transition from typewriter, was supposed to simplify our correspondence, creative writing, and research etc. But we did not realise that with this comes, annual upgrades, subscription to firewalls, anti virus software, occasional breakdowns, loss of data etc., all resulting in added work for its users. You may laugh because I am stretching this argument a bit too far. Any such gadget will add to maintenance efforts taking away some of our time. These must judiciously used, avoided if not required heavily. For instance many of us maintain at home small printer that we rarely use. Not only does it occupy space but also needs maintenance. In my life I have bought 3 such printers and in total may not have printed more than 100 pages in the last 10 years. Just calculating the investment alone the cost of printing each page is around 200 Rupees. Which could have been just 10 rupees a page if I would have walked up to a local cyber café. Some of us do want to maintain a printer for any emergency but it all depends upon what is the need of the individual.

In the Wisdom literature of the Hebrew Scriptures this thought is echoed in Ecclesiastes: 'This is all that I have learned: God made us plain and simple, but we have made ourselves very complicated' (Ecclesiastes 7:29; Good News Translation).

Fr Charles Cummings[7] proposes three 'Rs': Reduce consumption, Recycle, and Rely on local community to reduce the complexity to bring simplicity in our life. He also advises us rely on oneself be self-sustaining as much as possible.

If you agree with these thoughts then why not embrace some of them in your life, progressively.

Don't disrupt the pace of life often

Many a times we become impatient when rewards do not come as fast as we wish them to. We become impatient and try to expedite, leave the job or try some other business venture. Some times it may help, but at times it may lead to a situation of plucking the fruit too early, committing costly errors and leaving a task just before it was to mature. We all know the famous story in which a person got a goose which laid a golden egg, but only one every day. He wanted to get rich quick and then decided to kill the goose and see if it has more such concealed in its belly! In the process even he lost the regular supply of golden eggs as well. A Hindi couplet of Kabir

धीरे धीरे रे मना, धीरे सब कुछ होए
माली सींचे सौ घड़ा, ऋतू आये फल होए

[7]Christian Monasticism and Simplicity of Life, Fr. Charles Cummings, OCSO from Gethsemani III, May 2008.

This couplet of Kapbir espouses the virtue of natural pace and let things take time to mature. All tasks do need its own time to flourish and mature.[8] Nature also suggests that we allow time for all activities to take its own course. Certain tasks must be done at slow pace to relish the virtues as stated in this Sanskrit sholka

शनैः कंथा शनैः पन्था शनैः पर्वत लंघनम,
शनैः विद्या शनैः विर्त पंचातानी शनैः शनैः

It means keep doing slowly and steadily activities like walking, weaving the quilt, climbing mountain, gathering knowledge and accumulating wealth. Never rush theses five, don't expedite.[9] How true are these words from ancient text, which make you realise that disrupting pace rarely helps.

As I write these words, the TV channels are airing 'exclusive' videos of two senior government officers, a husband-wife pair, whose house is stashed with several millions of illegal cash[10] in their bedroom. These two officials were found to have accumulated a number of property worth over 500 crore, much more than their known source of income. The investigating Tax officials had to work in multiple teams using several currency counting machines to just account for the wads of currency notes stashed in carry bags or under the bed. The concerned couple must not have believed in earning wealth slowly and obviously have resorted to illegal means. They now will have to fight the law of the land and perhaps lead a slower and secluded life behind the bars.

Many of us get discouraged during the very first week of our new job, first day at a tourist spot or first month in a new educational

[8]*Dheere dheere re mana,dheere sab kuch hoy maali sinche sou ghada,rootu aaye phal hoy..* Noted fourteenth century Hindi poet Kabir. Translated it means It takes time for things to happen. A gardener pours hundreds of water pot but the tree bears fruit only when the season comes.

[9]shanaih panthaa shanaih kanthaa shanaih parvata langhanam. Shanaih vidya shanaih virt panchatani shanaih shanaih. Translated it means Five things should be done slowly, sewing, long distance traveling, climbing up the hill, learning and earning.

[10]The Hindustan Times , New Delhi 5th Feb 2010, http://www.hindustantimes.com/IT-raids-yield-crores-in-cash/H1-Article1-505512.aspx

course. We get restless, crave for an early change and try to rush things. We don't savour the gradual unfolding of each of these situations that is so central to our human life. We must let out life unfold slowly, a day at a time at its own pace. The other day I was asked a similar question from a young colleague of mine when he felt he is not getting promoted after two years at the same level. I advised him to expect his next promotion always in 3+ years. During this period just continue to work hard and demonstrate your capabilities. If you get a raise in 2 years you will be pleased. Instead if you expect promotions every year you will be always dissatisfied even if you get it every 14 months!

Unclutter your mind

Clutters are objects which have no immediate use, yet occupy useful space. Some of them are kept for emotional reasons, some other for future use that seldom happens. All clutter need upkeep, dusting, cleaning or re-arrangement over the years. In the same way we clutter up our mind with many not-so-useful thoughts that require upkeep, maintenance and nursing without any possible benefit. Let me pick up some thought-clutters that need to be thrown out of our mind they way we throw out object-clutters during annual cleaning exercise.

First on my list is Grudge. Many a times when we are treated shabbily, ignored, insulted or belittled, we hold a grudge against that individual. Some times we retort and make the deal equal. But it is like knifing someone because he has knifed me. But both ways it creates equal hurt to the other and leaves each other bleeding equally. When such incident happens to close friends, colleagues and relatives we end up holding a grudge against that individual. Every time we hear, interact or converse about him a bad feeling comes in our mind. In order to free our mind we need to throw out our grudge by a simple act of forgiveness or by offering apologies. The other day a friend of mine brought out the subject of holding a grudge against yet another friend. My advice to him was that in order to un-clutter his mind, just forgive him, call him up, say sorry to each other and then move on. The moment we throw our grudge we will get a lot of peace of mind.

Second on my list is Greed. We all want to possess certain things, material goods or otherwise. There is nothing wrong in having such a desire. But longing for them to an extent that it gets converted into greed is not right. Greed is a state when we want to recklessly assemble more and more of the same thing without any limit. Most people who get into the vicious cycle of acquisition and more acquisitions are primarily driven by greed. They shamelessly acquire wealth, properties that many generations will not be able to utilise.

History is full of tales of Kings and empire builders who expanded their kingdom out of greed for more power and territory and finally ended up being dejected. King Ashoka was one such example who renounced his ambition after witnessing massive loss of human life in Kalinga war. Ashoka finally embraced Buddhism and sent several of his emissaries in nearby countries to propagate the teachings of Buddhism. Remember Duryodhan of Mahabharata days that refused to dispense just five villages to Pandvas. This precipitated into the epic battle of Mahabharata, leading to decimation of his own clans along with thousands of others.

Excess of everything is bad, is an age old saying. This is true with greed also. This is one vice that drives people to gamble, risky investments in stock market, unhealthy competition and of course taking recourse to short cuts. My simple suggestion is just get away from greed.

Think Positive, Have Fun

Power of positive visualisation has been proposed by many people, authors and change masters. In our life as well we need to always visualise a bright future ahead of us which at times maybe hard to do. The age old saying that *whatever happens, happens for the good* should be taken in the right spirit to accept our present and look forward for future with all earnestness.

Many a times we miss an opportunity. If we have not put in enough effort then we must try harder with a renewed vigour. Despite this if we fail to get what we expected, let us not loose our

Story: Whatever happens, just happens for the good

There is an old fable about a king who was advised by his Guru that he should consider whatever happens, happens for the good. Being an all powerful king, he was reluctant to accept this sane advice and thought he could take control on events that were unfolding everyday in his life.

Once due to some accident he lost one of his fingers. He narrated this incidence to his Guru and advisor. His Guru's answer was same, 'Whatever happens, happens for the good!'

The king became very upset and annoyed by this answer. Instead of words of sympathy, here was a Guru who wanted him to feel good about his loss and celebrate his pain! Consequently the King imprisoned Guru for his true speak.

The Guru again mumbled, 'Whatever happens, it happens for the good'. The king ordered more rigorous punishment to the guru's prison term.

After few months the king went hunting and lost his way. In the process he was separated by his troupe. While wandering in the forest he was captured by aboriginal tribes who felt that he is one of the people from an alien land. As the story goes, they wanted to behead him as a sacrifice in front of their deity.

While the king was being prepared for the ritual, one of members of the tribal community noticed that the king has one of his fingers dismembered. As per the tribal custom, such an incomplete person cannot be offered as sacrifice. Accordingly, he was released and the king finally returned to his kingdom.

When the king returned back to his capital he straight a way went to the prison, set the Guru free and apologised for his sort sightedness. The King realised his folly and gave lot of gold and land to the Guru.

The Guru again said, 'Whatever happens, it happens for the good!'

heart, brood or be obstinate, instead try something else. The future may have something different, better and interesting in store for us, for sure.

Even the *Bhagavad Gita* mentions that

> *Whatever happened, happened for the good;*
> *Whatever is happening is happening for the good;*
> *Whatever will happen, will also happen for the good only;*
> *You need not have any regrets for the past.*
> *You need not worry for the future. The present is happening.*[11]

Many years ago I missed a job that I was very keenly aspiring for. I felt self-pity when I lost out where my close friends got through. Yet, several years later, I realised that the job, which at one point in time, I was so keen on taking up was not at all suitable for my personality. It would have been a disastrous choice for me. Destiny was kind enough to mould me into my current profession, adopted after few trials, which is far more suited to my simple creative, non-violent and people-friendly profile. I realised that whatever happened to me in my life, both success as well as failure were ultimately for my own good. I have since started to look at the silver lining in every cloud that comes my way as most of these clouds bring refreshing rains too.

Many a times we are in a situation when disappointment of not achieving something is felt too hard. We perhaps do not realise that there are many other opportunities that may now open up because an alternative is ruled out. I have always seen that with every

[11]जो हुआ, वह अच्छा हुआ, जो हो रहा है, वह अच्छा हो रहा है, जो होगा, वह भी अच्छा ही होगा। तुम भूत का पश्चाताप न करो। भविष्य की चिन्ता न करो। वर्तमान चल रहा है। ... श्री मद्भागवत गीता

disappointment something good and better comes up. However, it takes time to realise it.

My company at one point decided to close down a department that I was leading due to intra-departmental politics. I was too frustrated at that point in time. It appeared like the end of my career to me. To add insult to injury, I was asked to report to the manager with whom I had professional differences.

I started with huge disappointment in the following months but to my surprise the turn of events proved to be much more pleasing than what I would have expected. Those dark days forced me to look out for something else and come out of my comfort zone. In all honesty, today I thank that event and the people involved for giving a positive turn to my career! They may have had an ulterior motive but for me it was blessings in disguise. I took the event in my own stride. Instead of brooding or sulking I spent my time reading and gaining more knowledge and developing new skills. I invested my frustration in trying new opportunities, did extensive study of various subjects and finally found a new beginning that has catapulted my career in a different orbit. In fact decades later I went and thanked some of them with all my humility.

What does the flowing water do when its path is obstructed? It finds some other path either breaks the mountain or its banks as the case may be. The key in the metaphor is that 'flowing' is true for our life too. We have to flow in our days and months and find new paths and pastures without getting constrained by obstructions or two. Many significant changes to career have happened to people when they were put in a corner, denied promotion or sidelined for a coveted office. These visionaries strived to do something else, have succeeded and proved their baiters wrong. When the founder of Tata Empire Late J N Tata decided to establish a Steel mill in Jamshedpur during the beginning of 20th century Britishers laughed at him[12]. No one realized that the same Tata Steel would

[12]The Chief Commissioner for Indian Railways, Frederick Upcott, to say: "Do you mean to say that Tatas propose to make steel rails to British specifications? Why, I will undertake to eat every pound of steel rail they succeed in making." Source http://www.tata.in/aboutus/articlesinside/FX6UE!$$$$!cbFhc=/TLYVr3YPkMU= accessed 20032014.

buy Corus Steel a reincarnation of British Steel one day[13]. Most creative epics and great writings were generated when the writer /poet was pained, rejected or pushed to the brink. If you get an easy life will you try to do things differently? Perhaps you will not. It is said that no pain and therefore no gain hence accept the pain as part of life building process.

Let others help me and I will help others: Soon after his accident Jeeva discovered rather accidentally that he has large number of friends and well-wishers who cared for him immensely. He may not have lots of material or physical wealth but these emotional assets were un-perishable and pilfer proof. Even friends, whom he had not spoken for years, came to enquire about him, offered help and left a tip or two for his speedier recovery. All this helped him.

I remember a close relative of mine who was always ready to help others. For example he would volunteer himself to supervise someone's daughter's marriage arrangements or help someone's son find a decent job. He will be always be around and ready to support friends and relatives as the needed. Consequently he was nicknamed as 'Bahle admi' (Good person) and regarded as such by the close fraternity. We must volunteer to be of help to people who need our help, even though they may not explicitly have asked for. Pass a tip, drop a hint and make them comfortable to bring out their issues and reach out to us. Jeeva realised that he is being helped because he would have helped others in the past. He must also continue this practice in future so that the cycle of mutual support continues.

Just be yourself and don't punish yourself

> *'I gave up my struggle with perfection a long time ago........ be yourself, the day is about lot more........'—Anne Hathway, Hollywood Actor*[14]

[13]Tata steel bought Corus in 2007 source: http://www.tata.in/htm/Group_MnA_CompanyWise.htm?sectid=Mergers-and-acquisitions accesses 20032014

[14]Quoted in Female-first.co.uk, Source:*Delhi Times*,the *The Hindustan Times* magazine, 26th January 2010.

Story: A traveler was walking in intense heat and became tired and thirsty. He came near a tree which had wonderful shade and to his surprise he found a pitcher full of cool water. He drank some water to quench his thirst and sat under the shade to cool himself down. He found a hut nearby and went to the door and knocked. An old couple came out and offered him something to eat. As he continued his journey he realised that the way these people have planted a tree, kept a pitcher of water for travelers near their house, he should also do the same.

We don't plant tree in front of our house to sit under it, but for the travelers who pass by.

Some of us are not too happy about our own self. We incessantly judge ourselves by being overtly critical. Some of us feel bad about our appearance, height, colour of skin or just background, social status, etc. The moment someone points our shortcomings, we start believing their words and feel dejected. Such desire for approval from others will push us to the brink of catastrophe. Several impressionable young individuals as well as grown up ones, do take extreme recourse just because a friends, relative or office colleague has made a nasty comments about them.

Remember the negative opinion expressed may be due to several reasons. The person in question may be comparing you with others, his standards may be high or he may be just plain biased. Just consider these opinions as their perceptions and not a true reflection of your abilities. Do improve in areas where you are weak yet never get carried away by rejection, criticism and negative opinion. Just carry on in your stride unperturbed. No one would know more about the challenges of rejection than J. K. Rowling, the best-selling author of the *Harry Potter* fantasy series, which sold more than 400 million copies. Her manuscript was rejected by as many as 12 publishing houses.

Remember the old story of a painter who put up his painting for suggestions and comments on a street square. He requested passersby to put a cross where they felt the painting needs improvement and soon it was filled with crosses all over. So what if I am dark, short, fat or ugly? So what if I am not able to run faster or cannot swim? I am what I am and nothing can reduce my resolve to strive towards my own goal that I think I am capable off achieving. Living on borrowed praise from others makes one weak and yearn for more praise to feel good.

Several artists, creative personalities and sports persons do get initial rejection. They may have needed to improve their performance during those initial days like most of us do. But they did not accept their initial rejection as the final words for their life. They continued making efforts, decided to try harder with different people. They also must have improved themselves in the processes. With their resolve they reached phenomenal heights later in their career. A famous Bollywood actor who started his career in early 70's was considered too tall to be a popular hero for Hindi films but he proved his critics wrong by becoming the most admired actor of the century. He is still in demand after nearly forty years since those initial days of rejection. Another lady actor was considered too plum and dark to fit the acceptance criteria. Today after 30 years she is touted to be the timeless beauty even when she is well past in her fifty.

With recent incapacitation Jeeva knew very well that he will have to slow down in certain areas and have to limit the sky of his ambition somewhat due to his physical limitations. But it would be his choice as to what the limit he decides for himself. Accepting oneself in its existing form and loving in totally was an important step for him and any one who wants to lead a balanced peaceful life.

Osho Rajneesh says[15] that when we love ourselves only then can we can love others. Osho gives example of a pebble being thrown into a lake. The ripples will at first arise close to the pebble and then only can reach the shores. Preventing ripples to touch the pebble will also prevent ripple reaching the shore. Similarly loving yourself is a must

[15]*Love Yourself* (Paperback,1997) by Osho.

before loving others. When you love yourself you can meditate, be at ease with yourself and not carve for company and excitement always, says Osho. So love yourself and don't punish it even when you fail to realise any of your ambitions.

Jeeva got cheered up with this thought. He decided to implement this idea. He asked the nurse 'can you make me sit up please'. When she lifted the back rest of his bed he felt much better. He then looked at his reflection in the wall mirror in front of him. With several gadgets attached to his body, belt around his chest and slings in one hand, it was a marvelous sight. He combed his hair, shaved his beard, applied some soothing cream and then smiled at himself. He just accepted himself in whatever form it was. In future he decided not to feel bad even if he does not measure up to his own standards occasionally.

Must step: Stop procrastinating

The must step of any transformation journey is the first step. This is the most difficult yet the most important one. We hear numerous good thoughts but most of them remain dormant in our to-do list for action on some other day and that day never arrives. He decided that from now onwards he will stop procrastination. While he never allowed procrastination for his work related activities but actions related with his own self were often relegated for next weekend, next month even next year. All these included tasks related with the upkeep of his health, financial planning, devoting time on hobby and spending time with family. He realised that he had not taken a quiet vacation for several years. You too readers, if convinced, just take few actions before you read the next paragraph.

You must stop procrastinating about balancing your work life.

Live a day at a time

Few years later Jeeva was in different setting altogether. The audience comprised of the students, the budding managers, from a premier management school. Speakers after speaker were sharing their wisdom with the students espousing the virtue of great leaders, celebrities star, business tycoons and sports personalities. Everyone was heaping praise on the greatness of those icons, how they achieved great success and what all they did.

When Jeeva's turn came to speak he said 'I would not suggest you to look only up to the end state of these great people. Remember they would have spent years of hard toil before they reached their iconic status. I would rather suggest that don't just look at the pinnacle of their success but at the preceding steps that these individuals took without being noticed. Before his first test century that Sachin Tendulkar hit, there were hundred of days he spent playing league matches and school cricket final. Don't ignore what all he did before being an icon. If you walk only by looking up in the sky you will not take your next step properly and may fall in the impeding ditch. So just make best use of your today by addressing the task at hand wisely and efficiently, not in just dreaming for the glorious future for yourself. If you spent your day well, the ensuing week, month and the entire life will improve automatically.

Suppose you are engaged in study then do with all earnestness every day till you obtain your degree. If your job is to serve a customer, do it as if this is the first customer you have with utmost sincerity. If you are doctor attending a patient just attend to her needs with all professionalism at your command as if you have the power of God flowing through you to cure the person. In this process not only you would feel good about yourself but also deliver to the organisaisation, society and the community.

Doing a task with perfection, dedication with utmost care without making too much of publicity is the better way than bragging and boasting and finally achieving nothing. We recently saw that the hot favorite team participating in 2010 FIFA world cup, led by iconic coaches and supported by millions of slogan shouting fans could not even reach the semi final stage. This was no accident or sheer bad luck of the loosing side but the winning team simply achieved it through better planning, low noise preparation and focus on the game rather than worrying about garnering media footage.

There is a dialogue from an acclaimed Hollywood movie *'The day of heroes are pass, I maintain a low profile*[16] aptly sums up virtue of doing job quietly rather than bragging about it much before it is accomplished. The life of common people like most of us, you and me variety, who work in banks, retail chains, software companies or call centers, should not fall in the trap boasting what they do but doing efficiently and quietly what they are asked to do.

If I have to choose between praise and performance I would rather choose performance which is more lasting. In fact According to Naomi Aldort[17], children who are subjected to endless acknowledgment and praise eventually learn to do things not for their own sake, but to please others. Jeeva reminded students that the days of bragging super stars, talkative sportsperson and garrulous politicians have gone. Live you

Story: Day dreaming: There was boy who did some work for a farmer in the field. As reward for his work, the farmer offered him a glass of milk. Instead of drinking the milk there itself, the boy decided to carry it back home.

While walking back home he started to day dream as to what else he could do with the glass of milk. He thought that he might as well sell this glass of milk and earn some money. The money which he would get will enable buy him one or two eggs. He continued in his thought to explore further. Soon these eggs will get converted into chicken. This chicken will breed more chicken over time. When he will have sizeable number of chickens, he will sell them and finally buy a good horse for riding. As he was walking with the glass full of milk, he dreamt that one day he would ride the horse. And he did a mock trial of riding the imaginary horse while the glass full of milk was still in his hands. In this process he split the entire milk on the ground.

[16]A dialogue from the movie The Contract (2007) delivered by the main cast Morgan Freeman.

[17]Aldort, Naomi (2000?) "Getting out of the way" article available on http://naomialdort.com/articles3.html.

life a day at a time, make most of it, do dream but not so often that you forget to enjoy and do your duty of the day!

The moral of the story is that don't dream too distant of future and in the process spoil the gains of today. Even for the work life balance, plan for short term, try for few months and then revise often.

Be a good human being

Each one of us must embark upon a personal journey towards timeless goal of living a good life—(by) being a good human being—even as we tackle the world's largest problem[18]. ...... His Majesty king Jigme Khesear Namgyel Wangchuck, King of Bhutan

It was rather surprising to hear these thoughts from the youngest king of the tiny nation of the world, espousing the virtues of simplicity and being good human being to achieve higher *Gross National Happiness*. He was making his pitch to address global problems such as environment, ecology, pollution, terrorism and many others just by embracing the age old wisdom of 'be good to see good' around all of us.

In the current fiercely completive world where material possession is the criteria of one's success, an advice to be good human being looks archaic and out of place. Yet the realisation about collective issues the mankind is facing such as environmental chaos, economy instability, natural disasters and man-made security problems are proving to be insurmountable unless we change our thinking. In this context the thought of H.M. king Jigme Khesear Namgyel Wangchuck of Bhutan were refreshing. All these challenges have proved that the time has come to return to these thoughts of self-control, good behaviours and mindset changes that our ancient texts advocate. India is amongst the few countries that advocated the principles of Basudahiva *Kutumbakam*,[19]

[18]His Majesty king Jigme Khesear Namgyel Wangchuck, 29, while delivering the Madav Rao Scindia Memorial lecture, New Delhi, 23rd December 2009, *The Hindustan Times* 25th December 2009, page 9.

[19]The entire world is a family.

or as aptly written on the back of many trucks *Jeeyo aur jeene do.*[20] The time has come to return to these principles and follow them in totality.

Many of our current days problems of stress, tension etc., are brought about due to our petty greed of additional possession that we want to steal from our brothers, neighbors, friends, colleagues or fellow citizens. How can we expect a country collectively to behave differently as long as its citizens in their personal life have been amassing wealth by taking away from others! We see people encroaching upon others space literally as well as figuratively! People want to grab position or power in their day to day life. This behaviour is so pronounced in the high profile corporations, government departments and offices people plot and scheme to undermine colleagues, superiors or team members to gain few extra brownie points, a promotion or raise. One may doubt the relevance of the advice to follow a principled life in this world, because many people believe that *Nice Guy finish last.*[21] Even parents these days encourage their children to be fighter. The net result is that each one of us competes and grabs something from somewhere. No wonder we plunder environment, pollute rivers and also vitiated the atmosphere where we work! So if the entire world collapses due to our greed, will we survive?

Kaun Likhe ab Lambhi Chtti Chote sab samvad ho gaye
Sada jeevan achhi batein karma aab apradh ho gaye
Jood raha yeh antarjal, har jan ko har jan se jag mein
Ghrina dwesh aur dambh ke jale aub to sab ke pass ho gaye![22]

[20]Live and let others live.

[21]A popular phrase to depict the plight of being good. Also a hit song 'Nice Guys Finish Last', by Green Day, won an MTV movie award for the best song from a movie in 1999.

[22]A couplet by Sashandu translated it means.

No one writes long letters, just sends short messages, Plain living and good thinking has become a crime

World wide web is joining each one of us, but each one now full of cobwebs of greed, hate and arrogance!

Story: A simple story may be worth considering at this stage. Someone from the big world of business by accident landed up in a remote island. It was small beautiful place with folks milling around happily, few sky scrapers and the biggest sources of their earning was from fishing in the sea. 'How do you pass your day without having fast cars, big shopping malls and entertainment parks? I also don't see the buzz of high profile media?' He asked one of the contented looking individual.

'Well, we go out for fishing few days a week, come back with our boats full of fish that we sell in the near by market. Rest of the time we tile our small garden, grow vegetables, play with our children and take siesta in the afternoons'.

'But you could do more. You are wasting a big opportunity. You can buy big trawler boats and go to deep sea and net bigger ones.'

'So what will happen then?' asked the simple looking fisherman.

'Oh you don't realise what you are missing in your life. Once you catch big fish you can start exporting them by putting a processing plant and earn more money' The management expert was not amused with stoic silence and un inquisitive look at the listener's face.

'So what will happen thereafter?' the fisherman uttered few words.

'Well once you have enough money you can expand your business, go global by spreading your expertise and brand and even invite big private equity funds to invest.' The consultant added.

'I can see that but how will it help my life' said the simpleton.

'Once the strategic investments come they will create the market hype and lead it to make it public. You will get a large reward for your initial investments. You can choose to run the company or ...' consultant was expecting some interest in the fisherman but none was visible. Yet he stopped sensing that the fisherman has something to say.

'But what will do will all the money after so much of efforts and stress' he asked plainly.

'You don't seem to understand. Once you will have lots of money you can buy pieces of land in a quite village, enjoy your life with your family and occasionally go for your pet hobby fishing in your own boat'. The consultant was exasperated to find that the fisherman was not yet moved by his grand business vision. So he waited for the fisherman to reply.

'But this is what I am happy doing now' said the fisherman, doubting the wisdom of the new age consultant.[23]

Recently a massive tragedy in the upper reaches of Himalayas in the northern state of India led to the loss of thousands of human life due to cloud burst, massive flood and landslide. The TV footage showed the horrific tale of the survivors and the heroic efforts of our men in uniform from army, airforce and other security agencies. Life is too uncertain was proved once again and some of these uncertainties have been brought by us by playing with environment and viewing all activities of our life just through commercial lenses. There is no need to elaborate on what happened there but only to suggest that life is limited so do something that makes you worthy of its possession.

Self-control is the best control: The realisation is now slowly but surely setting amongst several thought leaders that self-control is the best way to make the world a better place to live. Unnecessary craving without realising that at the end we all want peace and tranquility in our lives has made many people return to their roots. Many busy executives have decided to take up less competitive jobs or assignments. They have taken up social cause such as setting up village schools, running social projects and even teaching. If each one of us becomes simple and peaceful the world will become as such. If each

[23]Story source: Anonymous.

one of us becomes a better person then the world would become a better place to live, no doubt.

Do you agree? If yes then make small efforts in this direction from now onwards, every day.

I will be failing in my duty if I touch the subject of work life balance by just telling few interesting stories and giving some nice sounding tips. You may use them occasionally to manage your task, time or tension at the work place. But that is just scratching the surface of a bigger problem. There are hundreds of such self-help books already available and one more would do no good. My endeavor is to share how some of these teachings were understood during those critical period in Jeeva's life and attempts that he made to take advantage of them. It was like the transformation journey for him, a 'eureka',[24] moment. I must add that these thoughts were life defining for him, something that his swelling bank balance or several material possessions could never do for him. These efforts were not from a failed or dejected individual to embrace compromise or a story of 'sour grapes'. As a matter of fact after practicing these thoughts he got a feeling of being a bird floating in the vast empty sky unhindered. However, if some of theses practices did not result in any benefit to him then the blame was entirely on the lack of persistence and implementation. Jeeva meanwhile continues to work on these aspects of his life to gain better work life balance and improve every day.

Let us examine some of the principles for work life balance that were so useful to usher the transformation in Jeeva's life.

Balance Body, Mind and Soul

> *The religion of the future will be a cosmic religion. It should transcend personal God and avoid dogma and theology.... Buddhism answers this description.... If there is any religion that could cope with modern scientific needs, it would be Buddhism.*
>
> —Albert Einstein

[24]Archimedes supposedly came out half naked from his bath tub shouting 'eureka' when he could crack the buoyancy principle. This is principle that is used to make boats, ships and aircraft which changes the meaning of travel.

Our existence is dictated by the combinations of three things. The first one is our body that we see and touch. The second one is our mind that allows us to think and act. Finally our invisible soul is the third one. Indian scriptures use the metaphor of body as a chariot driven by senses as the horses. It is the mind that reins the horse in the hands of the driver, the soul, which is also the master who directs our life[25]. So we are not just one but combination of these three elements that makes us all, not just the body alone.

In order to balance our life we need to think and act for each one of these. Like the chariot our body needs rest, repair and rejuvenation. The sensory horses need gratification, entertainment and sensual fodder to run the race of our life. But it is the mind that needs to control the overbearing senses. Mind must be conditioned and educated to lead us to the right direction. Finally there is an invisible soul that binds them all. Our soul (atma), according to Indian scriptures is eternal and completely different from the perishable physical body. Krishna in the epic *Bhagvat Gita* says that soul never dies.

> नैनं छिन्दन्ति शस्त्राणि नैनं दहति पावकः ।
> न चैनं क्लेदयन्त्यापो न शोषयति मारुतः ।।२३।। .. श्रीमद्भगवद्गीता[26]

It says that Soul is immortal and carries with it the good or bad deeds in the current life to the next one.

I am not entering in a debate of reincarnation and similar such theories. A simple explanation of this sholka is that the good or bad deeds of a person do remain visible beyond their life time. Paintings of renowned artists, piece of literature, even contributions of leaders, scientists, architects, business luminaries does evoke positive response which can be attributed of carrying you good deeds beyond you life. And the reverse is also equally true that bad deeds will be remembers for long and despised.

[25]See http://www.adi-shankara.org/2008/02/this-body-is-chariot.html.

[26]Krishna says in Chapter 2 verse 23 of the epic *Gita* referring to the soul, Weapons can nit cut it nor the fire burn it, neither wind can dry it nor water can wet it.

In summary, a true balance can only be achieved in a healthy body, sound and calm mind and pious soul. These three are so intertwined that just by keeping one in good state is not enough. All these three are like, three legs of a tripod, only one or two will not make it stand as shown in Figure 4.2

How do we take care of Body, Mind and Soul Together?

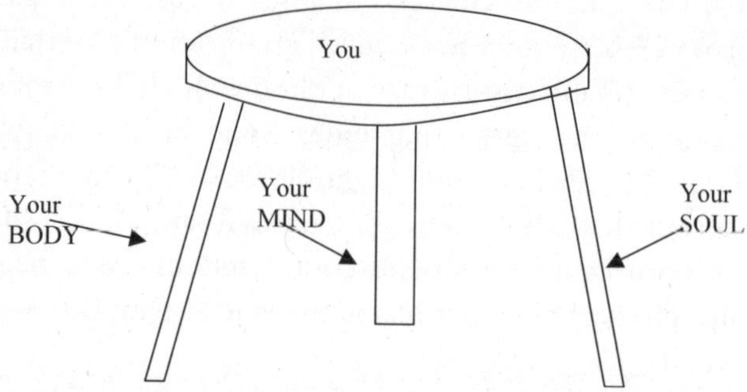

Figure 4.2 Three constituents of a human being

An Indian couplet says *Bhooke bhajan Na hohi Gopala.*

This couplet means that we can not prey with empty stomach. We need to have a sound an healthy body to pursue anything in life. Whether it is intellectual, material, social achievements or spiritual accomplishment, all these can only be delivered through a healthy body. There is a good trend these days towards upkeep of body through exercises, weight training, beauty treatment and health care. But caring for body alone is not enough. A beautiful body must house a sound and balanced mind that is governed by a spiritual soul.

A strong urge for action enveloped Jeeva's mind leading him to these soul searching questions.

- *Is he taking enough care of all of these or just for few of them?*
- *Is he travelling towards a destination following the right path or is he just sitting on a stationary chariot doing nothing and feeding his sensory horse nice fodder which is taking him no where?*
- *Is he accumulating credentials which will last beyond his life time? Simply*

speaking, is he doing good deeds that people would remember and find use of when he is not around?

He did not want to be in the category of people who are self-centered, who come in this world for self-gratification and leave a trail of destruction behind without giving anything worthwhile to the people behind.[27]

Gita says that our five aggregates: body, feelings, perception, predispositions and consciousness, constantly change. If we follow a path of right view, right thought, right speech, right action, right mode of living, right endeavor, right mindfulness, and right concentration, life would be full of bliss. Jeeva decided that he would follow these principles but was still having doubts about whether he could do it.

Balance your life: Follow Madhya Marg

> *Giving life without claiming authority, benefiting without demanding gratitude,*
> *guiding without control. This is called hidden virtue.*
>
> —*Lao Tzu, 6th century BC sage*

Jeeva took a cue from the teachings of the Buddha to develop his life based on balanced middle path. It was the great saint Gautam Buddha[28] who preached Madhya Marg, (Middle Path) for a virtuous and balanced life. This is a right path to be followed not only in the personal lives of individuals but in social relations, in work situation or economy, politics or international relations. Since our focus of this book is help individuals achieve their work life balance, our inferences from this philosophy will in this context alone.

The Buddha says that one must practice:

- Love for all human beings
- Generosity: the art of giving to others

[27]कुछ किये भी नहीं और कुछ दिए भी नहीं, आये खाए पिए और मैला छोड़ कर चले गए. A popular Village saying which means that you did nothing gave nothing and left leaving lot of dirt behind.

[28]Buddha means the *awakened one.*

- Contentment within the available means
- Truthfulness, observe and uphold truth in all interactions and dealings
- Awareness and mental clarity

Yet Buddha does not advocate us to follow blindly all these just because someone says so. He advocates us to observe and analyze these thoughts reflect and contemplate and when you are convinced then only accept it and live up to it. Only then you will realise how your pleasure is converted into bliss. Like all simple teaching these simple ideas are rather difficult to implement. But they are not impossible if you and I have resolved to walk this path.

It was a refreshing change Jeeva found in his thinking being moulded by these simple prescriptions. He was now truly approaching his relationship with known and unknowns with a sense of love and desire to give. When he regretted a job offer he volunteered to help the selection board with possible names that could fit the role criteria easily. 'But why would you do it?' The HR VP of the prospective firm asked him in disbelief. 'Because I met you and must leave behind some positive feelings' Jeeva said adding more to VP HR's skepticism.

Being content within his means and speaking truth as often as possible was making him feel calm and tranquil. He felt he was becoming more aware of himself with absolute clarity of his mind as if a new dawn was descending from the horizon.

What Gurus have to say

The quest of finding the right balance of various aspects of life also led Jeeva to various Gurus and their teachings. To Jeeva, all of them appeared to advice almost the same. Like most good advice the effect of good advice is not in the advice but in confirmatory actions, reflections, assimilation and suitable correction thereafter.

For example the following steps based on noted Guru H.H. Sri Sri Ravi Shankar discourse gave him a summary[29] to adopt a well balanced posture in his lives.

[29]Based out of one of his discourses, exact one can be obtained from his website. http: / / srisriravishankar.org/ Ed: please provide the url details for this website.

1. Thank and be grateful to God for all that he has given us, food, water, air, life and so on.
2. Take out time to think, meditate and reflect at a quiet place every day.
3. Understand that our life is impermanent and therefore understand the futility of worrying about small gains or amassing material objects that will loose their sheen sooner or later.
4. Don't leave an opportunity to act kindly to people without any expectation for a return favour. These small steps will make world a better place to live.
5. Smile often, share it with strangers. It will not only help you increase your confidence but also to spread the happiness around.
6. Meditate regularly even if it is for 10–15 minutes. Try doing it at an appointed time whenever possible, though early mornings are the best.
7. Use some time to do short breathing exercises, and yoga as well.
8. Cultivate the sprit of a learner and adapt student-like behaviour, which will add something new every day and keeps you on the course of correction.

Be a student always: Student like behaviour also allows one to respect others, big or small from whom you can pick up an idea or two and be grateful. Jeeva remembered several small messages form friends, colleagues and several noted people in casual discourses or writings or even strangers have made far greater impact on changing his thinking and behaviour. However, for learning from someone we must respect that individual, be humble to listen and thankful for his advice. You will see that with this demeanour the outlook of your life does change a lot.

Control your anger and dedicate your energy to love

> *Anyone can become angry—that is easy, but to be angry with the right person at the right time, and for the right purpose and in the right way—that is not within everyone's power and that is not easy.—Aristotle*

Anger is the most damaging and destructive trait that spoils our work life balance. We become angry when we face a situation or behaviour that we don't like or are unpleasant. We become angry because we fail to accept things as they are, with a hope that we will be able to change it through our anger. At times it does, when we show our anger to an errant child or worker, but think of the damage it does to your own self. You might have noticed that when you are angry not only your inner peace is lost but anger also generates harmful toxins which damages the body systems slowly. While the reason of anger ranges from disappointment, being cheated, not able to address fear to being sad, feeling helpless or just left out, all situations are arising out of two reasons:

1. Not being able to accept the situation.
2. Not being able to do anything about it.

Uncontrolled anger leads to aggressive behaviour causing greater damage to our own self than to the person on which the anger is directed. Several research studies have brought out physical and mental damage uncontrolled anger brings to individual. High blood pressure, strokes and violent attacks are just few of them.

Gaining mental peace to balance our life can only be achieved if we control our anger. We should channelise our displeasure through some constructive means and stay away from aggression. Whenever you feel like getting angry, take some time to think, cool down a bit, keep yourself in the other person shoes, forgive if the error is minor and only react to help the other guy correct the mistake for future. In no case get angry from in side but only through your words. These simple steps will help you to control you behaviour.

Anger avoidance does not mean non-action

Avoiding anger does not mean avoiding action to correct a mistake. One can censure, admonish, penalise and sentence the person making mistake without being angry. Remember the dialogue of Akbar from the movie Jodha Akbar where he simply says 'drop him from the high wall repeatedly till he is dead' to his errant step brother who was bent upon defying his authority. Akbar disliked his step brothers' behaviour and issued the death sentence without being angry.

In fact those of us who seldom get angry wield far more authority than one who shouts at every provocation. Just look around your own environment and you can distinguish between cool, calm and strong personality as compared shouting and ranting yet unsure ones and the timid or meek those have no voice at all. My prescription is to adopt the first one. Have you every heard a Lion King of jungle roaring at every movement of any object? Its mere presence and mild growl is enough to send a chilling shiver down the spine for many. Even if it finds errant ones, it will pounce and kill but without being angry. I recall my senior Mr Kapadia who would have never shouted at any one yet had great command over the team and people. If he would simply say 'I am not happy' the person concern would feel that he has done the biggest mistake of his life and no one would come forward to condone him. In his farewell speech after working for 30 years Mr Kapadia said 'a lot of people told me that I would be chewed up in the big bad industrial world with my simple non-aggressive style, but I can certainly say today that they were all wrong'. Gandhi ji also says that *whenever you are confronted with an opponent; conquer him with love and the policy of an eye for an eye will only end making the whole world blind.*

Have faith, trust and devotion

> There is no fire like greed,
>
> No crime like hatred,
>
> No sorrow like separation,
>
> No sickness like hunger of heart,
>
> And no joy like to joy of freedom.
>
> Health, contentment and trust, are your greatest possessions,
>
> Look within.
>
> Be still. Free from fear and attachment,
>
> Know the sweet joy of living in this way.—from the Dhammapada[30]

[30]http://www.beliefnet.com/Quotes/Buddhist/Dhammapada/F/From-The-Dhammapada/There-Is-No-Fire-Like-Greedno-Crime-Like-Hatred.aspx accessed 20032014.

Irrespective of what all we do to balance our work life, live happily, purposefully and responsibly, we will hit occasional road blocks. Like the patchy stretch on a highway, we have to slow down, manage the detour and then come back again to continue our efforts for leading a balanced life. During all these phases we have to keep our faith, trust and devotion.

Remember the phrase in the event of an adversity (or even when you are upbeat and happy): *This too shall Pass*,[31] to keep the faith that future will always be bright![32] A question was asked to a saint as to why God does not come immediately when we need him. The saint said 'when you go to a fair with your child he starts running around but does not feel lost as he knows you will come back and hold him when he needs you and you always do. Similarly God is around and will come to our help when we need him, have faith trust and devotion. His help may not be exactly in the way what you dream off but will come in a form to show other doors if one of them is closed.'

The new age wisdom has put lots of unnecessary questions in our minds. We doubt everything, everyone and all the teachings just because we want to see a proof ourselves. But we cannot lead our life by only asking questions but have faith that we will find answer to our problems. We have to keep trying to get beyond these questions.

प्रश्नों से में घिरा हुआ होऊं खोज रहा हूँ उनके उत्तर
फिर खुद से कुछ प्रश्न पूछ कर हो जाता हूँ और निरुतर
फिर भी मैं करता प्रयास हूँ[33]

.. सशंदु

[31]'This too shall pass', is a phrase occurring in a Jewish wisdom folktale involving King Solomon.

Also a poem by Helen Steiner Rice of which some lines are quoted below:

Then nothing in life can defeat me, for as long as this knowledge remains
I can suffer whatever is happening, for I know God will break all of the chains
For there is no night without dawning, and I know that my morning is near.

[32]One of my seniors, Mr A.K. Mukherjee, used to always say this to encourage us.

[33]Translated it menas ... I am surrounded by questions and trying to find their answers, yet few questions come up in my own mind, all I can do is try.

Finally try to attain freedom

> *What will matter is not what you learned, but what you taught others.*
>
> —Anonymous

> *Noted guru, J. Krishnamurti*[34] *says one must have freedom both outwardly and inwardly. Without freedom there is no clarity on what you want to achieve in life. When you are free from all bondage and restrictions you can find and give true love; find truth and go beyond the limitation of the mind.*

Look at any child and you will see how much free the child is. He sleeps where ever and whenever he feels like. Suddenly starts to play, asks questions, gives unrestricted comments and does things to her liking. Any one year old that has barely learnt to walk and talk is more free than most of us. A balanced life is a step towards this state of freedom. Most creative people behave freely; do what they think they want. Similarly, those organisations that want greater return from their employees, distribute more freedom to them such as to choose type of work, seating space, working hours, projects or teams. Most start-ups have a collegial environment and grant freedom of work amongst its team members. Everyone is treated equally to contribute and the rewards are shared equally. The phenomenal growth of Google in the IT business space is also due to its curiosity laced playroom like culture; where a new entrant is asked to design his/her own work area Freedom always leads to creativity and less stress. Even established corporations like IBM allow a lot of freedom of flexibility to choose mentor, career option and work schedules. In Indian corporations Tata steel, Hero group and many others give lot of employee freedom. All this leads to better employee contribution, less attrition and long term stickiness with their employer.

Freedom also means enjoying the fruit of your labour. A bird flies up to a certain level and then spreads the wings, relaxes and just glides

[34]J. Krishanmurti, Bombay, India, January 1968 *Collected Works*. Vol. VIII. Ed: please provide the complete title details AC added.

in the air. We all see them once in while and can feel how good they must be feeling. The state of freedom is attained when knowledge of self (atman gyanam) reaches at stage of maturity. Earning a living, attaining more and more power or position, relentless hard word, or even continued learning and gathering more degrees, diplomas and books must somewhere culminate into a happy feeling of having 'arrived'.[35]

While climbing the uphill path of life one must occasionally stop when reach a plateau, and enjoy the beautiful view of the surroundings. Stop where you can freely enjoy the environs. The top most point may not give the best view nor can give stability to stay there for long!

Summary of key themes

1. Four simple steps for work life balance:
   a. First define what you want to achieve realistically in life.
   b. Assess the extent to which your current role /job is meeting these needs.
   c. Decided to prioritise the key areas for action.
   d. Draft a plan of action.
2. Take the work life balance quiz to ascertain your current situation (provided in Chapter 11).
3. First define your life goals under these heads and your plan of action for next 5 years (use Annexure B in Chapter 11).
   a. Artha, (money) financial goal.
   b. Dharma (Karma) your duty.
   c. Kama (enjoyment, sensual pleasure)
   d. Mokhsya (leaving a legacy or giving back to society).
4. Trigger the change in your life through action.
5. Start managing you day using the FLIP model.
6. Simplify your life by:
   a. reduced transaction overload,
   b. speaking the truth,

[35]'Stabilize on your "truest interest": Cosmic Uplink',, K. Vijayraghvan, *The Economic Times*. New Delhi 8th February 2010.

c. having fewer but solid relationship,
d. removing noise, and
e. using technology judiciously.

7. Do not disrupt the pace of life very often.
8. Unclutter your mind.
9. Think positive, Have fun.
10. Develop a helping attitude.
11. Just be yourself and don't punish it too much.
12. First step: stop procrastinating.
13. Live a day at a time.
14. Be a good human being.
15. Balance your life following the middle path.
16. Balance Body, Mind and Soul.
17. Control your anger and dedicate this energy to love.
18. Have faith, trust and devotion.
19. Finally realise yourself, attain freedom.

Please use Annexure L. of Chapter 11 Monitor your work life Progress to track your progress for next 30–60–90 day cycle.

CHAPTER FIVE

Recharge YOUR WORK

Pleasure in the job puts perfection in the work.

—Aristotle (384 BC–322 BC)

From confusion to clarity

Life for Jeeva was till then a series of uncoordinated actions. The preceding years of his life have been trying and tabulation, examining various options for education, career and of course building and supporting his family. He made choices that seemed to be handy and in vogue at that point in time but most of them failed to meet his personal self-aspiration in the long run. 'Net dissatisfaction in his life' was a summary that he would write for himself. At least this year should be better, his friend WSG said some times while sharing similar predicament in a discussion some years ago. If the job was good, the company had no desire to be in that business for long. If he did well in the job, the factors such as economic climate, 9/11 events, dot.com burst etc., worked against him. Then he would be forced to scout around for the next opportunity. Some other time while doing very well in his assignment, he would be denied the necessary reward and recognition for some strange factors that some of us called as 'luck'. At these situations he would be lured by other prospective companies with tall promises but most of them would be no different than the company he just decided to leave.

He was like a playful child he was picking up one toy and dropping other. He was akin to a student who was enrolling in one course of study but getting disenchanted soon enough to switch to other. He was like a fickle minded reader who loved to buy several books while on a visit to the book store, not sure which one he wanted to read first. He was getting discouraged fast and always impatient to jump. Similarly he was much interested in networking, meeting new people in seminars and get-togethers, adding to their list of friends but not nurturing the old ones enough.

But when he reached out to many of his contemporaries with this confusion he found that his not the only person. He was a reasonable representation of a modern age professional.

Does my value system match the organisation where I work?

At this juncture, when Jeeva had seen many cycles of job changes, he started getting a sense of clarity on what type of work environment he wanted during this forced period of inactivity. Considering that similar problem would exist in all organisations with some minor variation, he decided to find a balance in his work life by looking at an organisation that is closer to his personal value systems. Like when you want to settle down to live anywhere, you first select the city and the neighborhood. Once a locality is selected, you look for the right size and location of the house to live in. Selecting an organisation was like deciding about the locality. The right role was akin to finding a suitable dwelling to live in, something that one can change once he is part of the neighborhood. In his past he was too uncomfortable while working on a high profile roles with inflated perks in organisation with employee unfriendly policies. He judged the current organization where he worked on various parameters to find how closer it is to his value system. Fortunately he was comfortable in the organisation where he was which gave him a sense of relief. He would now be less edgy to find opportunity outside and try to navigate his career within the same company were he worked.

Clarity to consolidate

The very thought of savouring and enjoying what you already have appealed to him immensely. He realised that time has come when he need not strive to accumulate more but follow a philosophy of contentment. He must not try to rush while traversing the life's journey so that he can look around from the window the beautiful surroundings of its path. For him now the life was not hankering for reaching a destination as soon as possible but a journey to be enjoyed in its every moment.

Look at your work holistically: The 'I' framework

The important part of work life balance efforts is to find a job that you enjoy or try to enjoy the job what you have. Both are difficult to implement but efforts must be made nevertheless. But it will take time to achieve all that a person wants to have. Jeeva contemplated a simple model for the career progression, further explained by using the metaphor of capital letter 'I'.

Most of us start our career exploring various choices. While sampling many choices, one may find some good and some not so good. But a time comes when one has to concentrate on one or few choices that are closer to their liking. Once this choice is found one should stick with it, devote their time and energy to develop deep knowledge and capability in the chosen area.

Our initial years of our career are full of curiosity and discovering something new. This represented by the horizontal line at the bottom of the capital letter 'I'. As we progress we like something or find success with on which we want to focus our attention on and excel. We need to concentrate on that role or profession which we like as shown by the vertical line in the letter 'I'. It could be a role in an organization that is meeting my profile or a business venture that has become successful after trying few.

Once a sufficient degree of depth in terms of capabilities, expertise or business success is achieved, then one should try to diversify and add more capabilities as depicted by the top horizontal line of the letter 'I' at the top. The top horizontal line also represented the spread to share and apply what you have gathered with newer situations and opportunities. However, as life progresses at its own pace one must transition from one phase to the other at an opportune time. Be is the quest for knowledge, establishing career progression or managing business the metaphor of the letter 'I' represents it very well.

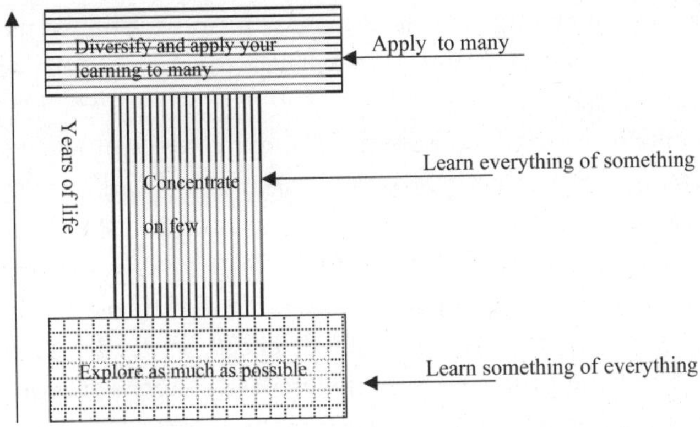

Figure 5.1 I—Metaphor for Managing Career

Craft your career

> A career mentor asked a simple question to the participants in a workshop?
>
> How many of you are managing or worrying or thinking about career of others?
>
> The participating group comprised of few seasoned executives and managers. Few sporadic hands were raised in the auditorium full of people.

> Then he said 'Good. Now tell me how many of you feel that someone else is managing and worrying about your career?'
>
> There was silence in the room; no one raised his or her hand.
>
> 'That is why you have worry about your career.
>
> Only you can craft you own career'.

As noted in the story no one else will worry about and will take actions about your career. It may be true that family members, parents and elders do remain concerned and may offer their good wishes or advice but they will not be able to help us manage it. So, each one of us have to think about our own career. We will have to take necessary action from time to time.

Should we be always obsessed about our career and solely focus on that?

No, not on a minute to minute basis for sure. You should not be so excessively concerned that your immediate tasks get affected or your work life balance is impacted. Your career is like a plant you have in your garden that needs to be tended, fenced, watered, supported, guarded and also protected from the predators. Above all, you have to love it and feel good when it blossoms and also take care when it is hit by a storm. You will have to nurture it so it grows and bears fruit. If you become obsessed every minute that it is not bearing fruit, poke it many times and it will decay. Remember everything takes time to grow and your career too will take time to grow. Follow a balanced approach.

However, at managed intervals taking proactive steps toward your career planning and its rejuvenation is necessary. This is to prepare you from any uncertainty, something that the fast changing world of economics and business is increasingly brining to our doors. Barring few jobs like that of government services where the career progression is dependent on the years you put in, most others like in the private sector, the progress depends on your merit, efforts and opportunities at hand. Even government positions at higher echelons are entrusted based on competitive evaluation. Irrespective of the sector, organisation or country (now most jobs are becoming global) the thoughts expressed in this book are useful and summarised after deep research, field interviews, personal experiences and observations. Adopt them what makes sense to you and get benefit from them using your own judgment.

Managing your career does not necessarily mean getting multiple promotions and becoming a CEO or Director at the age of 32! Career is a compendium of professional achievements, job satisfaction, monetary rewards, peer recognition and opportunities to give back to the society. That is why the word 'crafting' has been used while depicting career management to underline that unique approach is needed for each one of us for his / her career. Let us summerise some of the prevalent thoughts on career management and actions that we may take from work life balance perspective.

Constantly renew your career

The earlier understanding of career was centred on the paid employment that a person used to have throughout his life. In the current context it encompasses all related assignments that increase importance and reward-enhancing skills for the individual. A career is shaped trough education, training, work assignments, employment as well as direct or indirect activities performed within the enterprise, professional community, voluntary and leisure activity.

Since current age corporate do not guarantee us life time employment, employees too do not have loyalty for life with a single corporation. An average professional in America changes at least 5–9[1] jobs and India about 4–8 jobs. This trend is increasing for new age sectors such as IT, telecom and banking where staying with one company for more that 5 years is considered to be a stigma of sorts. Such frequent changes may not be healthy from work life perspective, but you decide what way you want to live your life because pains and pleasure will be ultimately yours.

[1]A report Source http://www.forbes.com/sites/jeannemeister/2012/08/14/job-hopping-is-the-new-normal-for-millennials-three-ways-to-prevent-a-human-resource-nightmare/ Accessed 20032014.

All of us have be cognizant of the fact that the business and economic environment is constantly changing, therefore it is our responsibility to manage our career and make us relevant and employable with the changing times. In these circumstances a constant enrichment and renewal of our career and job content is necessary. While some organisations do give opportunities for career enrichment and growth, it is our responsibility to select the right career choices which gives avenues for skills enhancement leading to career growth. Even in a highly evolved organization with good HR practices the onerous is always on the employee to navigate and promote his/her career through the labyrinthine of management layers by demonstrating his capabilities, reaching out for assignment and networking to get noticed.

Despite of best efforts some times we may reach a situation when the stagnation would set in. In such case growing horizontally, that is, taking up assignments of different types even though the level or emoluments remain the same is a better option. This gives opportunity to learn something new and different which will help recharge our career and grow ultimately.

Everyone wants to increase his/her income and also wants to do a better job with higher responsibility. While at the initial stages opportunities of growth may come from within the organisation boundary but at later stages one may be forced to change jobs. However, this will impact other aspects of life such as relocation woes for the family. Some times job changes are triggered due to corporate flattening, outsourcing, mergers and acquisition. In every such situation one has to prepare to bring the enthusiasm back in the work through increased participation, cross learning through his/her own efforts.

Remember, if you start preparing for your next job, even when you are fully comfortable and entrenched in the existing one, then only you can have the momentum to undertake a new situation. When the battery of your car is fully drained out its recharging would not work. Recharging must happen much before this stage is reached. A planned effort for crafting you career will ensure that every job move is with a long term objective in mind, suits the family responsibilities and is not just taken up because it offered higher package or there was nothing else available at that time! This effort in planning also helps to find what is wrong with the current career and what makes it less satisfying.

Consider your Life as a series of S Curves

A life is nothing but a series of interspaced 'S' curves. We start some where, go up the growth curve but then hit the plateau followed by a decline. So what do we do, accept this as a fait accompli or try to prevent the decline by hook or by crook, or instead do something differently? The smartness is to start another **S** curve much before the decline starts and pursue the next one to chart out a different course.

If you see the **s** curves in Figure 5.2, you will notice that hitting a plateau and decline is inevitable in any job or profession, role or responsibilities or business ventures. The next S curve which depicts your next move acts as safety net in case you have already initiated it. Every time when you jump from one S curve to the next, you have to reinvent yourself before the existing one hits the plateau. One must therefore start to think, plan and act for the next S-curve much before the current one hit the plateau. There is no point stagnating endlessly at a job, role or responsibilities if it is not meeting your work life aspirations. Do something new, different and unique and leave the past behind to move on to the next phase. As aptly said in a Hindi song:

Voh afsaana jise anjaam tak laana na ho mumkin
Use ek khoobsoorat mod dekar chhodna achchha[2]

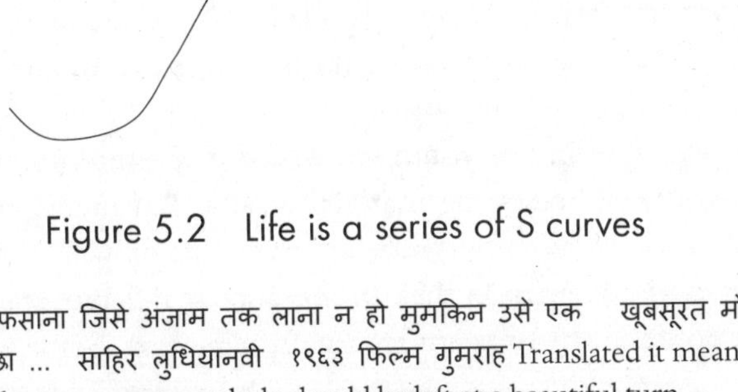

Figure 5.2 Life is a series of S curves

[2]वो अफसाना जिसे अंजाम तक लाना न हो मुमकिन उसे एक खूबसूरत मोड़ देकर छोड़ना अच्छा ... साहिर लुधियानवी १९६३ फिल्म गुमराह Translated it means.. The story which you can not conclude should be left at a beautiful turn..

For Jeeva too, like many others, the entire career was a culmination of several small yet related changes. He was hired to work as a maintenance engineer in a large process plant. But soon an opportunity came his way to join IT department as the management wanted to deploy IT for plant applications and needed engineers with relevant experience. Similarly at one point when he was engaged in a start up organisation, he found much pleasure to teach occasionally in business schools, a hobby that yielded him another s–curve as a weekend engagement in his life.

If you also look around, you will find that many people have made useful changes at regular interval to move from one role to the other effortlessly and to their unique advantage. There are several sports personalities who have turned commentators, several film personalities, doctors or lawyers have made a mark in politics.

Why can't we do the same to renew our careers?

Does the approach of work life balance change at various stages of our life?

During our life's journey we undertake different roles and responsibilities as we grow from being a child, youth to middle age and finally get old. Accordingly our priorities do change but not the fundamental make up of our different responsibilities. All the four segments of a balanced life, Artha, Dharma, Kama, Mokshya that will lead to self-actualisation is equally important as we pass through different stages of our life. Yet depending upon the stage of life some aspects would be more prominent than the other.

For example in our youth we would give more importance to enjoyment and possessing material wealth. But managing finance would be as much importance at later years as well. Other three segments would grow in their importance at different stages of life but at no stage any of them are totally irrelevant. Some avenues of enjoyment would find more merit in later years than what they used to be in earlier years.

Different Age: Different ways

Ancient Indian tradition envisages life into four stages called *ashramas*:

- Brahmacharya or the Student's life
- Grihasta or the Householder's life
- Vanaprastha or the life of a Hermitage
- Sanyasa, that is to Renunciate

Over the years the relevance of all these stages have somewhat been blurred as most of us neither believe nor follow them. We even laugh at someone who tries to bring this subject up in a conversation. But for Jeeva, this framework seems to be very interesting and relevant in the present times. He felt that if most people start following these ancient prescriptions and adopt behaviours commensurate to these stages of life, much of the modern social problems can be contained. While our lifestyles may have changed since then, the basic idea of these four stages is as relevant as it was in the past. The purpose for life planning is to direct all our energy towards ultimate self-realisation. For this goal, the understanding of these ancient thoughts in modern context will be helpful.

When we are at our first stage of life we need to learn how to manage our future as a student. Our studentship not only should be limited to gaining knowledge or degrees that facilitate livelihood but larger aspects of life such as managing family and community responsibilities and other subjects like health care and spiritual practices.

Our second stage of Grihasta/Householder phase corresponds to our productive and family life during which we try to attain worldly interests and meet worldly demands. Somehow this phase seem to go on and on. In the modern world people desire to continue this phase in perpetuity. If the person starts religious or spiritual practices during this period, however small it may be, it would not be impossible for him / her to prepare for the next stage. Politicians, film personalities and businessmen seem to distaste the very idea of calling it a day and continue to hanker this phase of life, only to realise its futility at the later years.

Vanaprastha / Hermitage in the modern context is a phase of life when one should redirect energy towards inner self. Taking recourse of increased spiritual practices of meditation, contemplation, and prayer comes in handy in this effort. The baton of worldly duties is increasingly passed to the next generation (in the family as well as at the place of work). The role must change from being a player to become a helpful coach and mentor. Attempt to simplify the life and consolidate your needs are undertaken. Also is the time when one must plan for retirement and discover what way he can plough back or give back to his community. The ambition should get replaced by satisfaction,[3] competition by cooperation and arrogance with humility.

The last phase which supposedly begins around 70 years (23–25 years for each of these life stages as per the ancient scriptures) is largely mis-understood amongst the modern clan. It is not expected in the modern times to take to sanyas in a retreat in the forest due to several reasons. Our life style, dependence on amities and health care may need us be in cities or closer to our families. Yet this is a stage when one must stop chasing worldly goals and seek self-actualisation and spiritual goals. The best vocation is to become teacher for others to make them understand larger aspects of life. This is the phase one should give back the accumulated wisdom. Ironically, we see people with ambition to overpower others, whose greed consumes grace and they chase a few remnant drop of life elixir. In this process they end up making fool to themselves.[4] Renunciation means not hankering for something, the time of which has passed, leave aside worldly possessions even lounging for respect and awards must be left at

[3]*"Where ambition ends happiness begins."—Source Unknown.*

[4]"In a Hierarchy Every Employee Tends to Rise to His Level of Incompetence." Dr Laurence J. Peter and Raymond Hull The Peter Principle, Buccaneer Books (February 1993).

this stage and time be devoted towards creativity, self-realisation and spiritual pursuits and prayer.

Work life Challenges of the internet age for different age groups

Last 10–15 years have been tumultuous and have brought phenomenal changes in our work settings and family life. The economic boom, opportunities galore and above all improved communication has made our personal life look exciting. In this process performance expectations have increased from each one of us from work, family, friends or colleagues. More communication devices mean more communication, expectation of faster turn around and increased infringement on our personal time. These challenges have made the life complex for all age groups at varying degrees. Let us see how it has effected various age groups and how we can the establish work life balance in our life.

At one end of the age spectrum are tender teens who are students and young professionals taking their first career steps, followed by young couples, with or without kids. There after are individuals who have reached mid career age and are juggling with multiple responsibilities. Finally we have two last categories; one being matured-career individuals and other retired or semi retired ones. Irrespective of the culture, country, religion or age this simple framework is immensely valuable for life planning. Even if we are introduced to these thoughts at later stage of our life and may have spent several years behind, just changing course for future would be a great achievement. A brief interpretation of priorities at each one of the following life stages are given in the subsequent paragraphs.

- Tender teens
- Twinkling twenties
- Thriving thirties
- Mid career
- Matured career
- Retried or semi-retired

Tender teens: The teen age years are the most interesting as well as challenging phase of our life. Full of potential but some times, if not managed well, can lead to a life time disaster. The chances are that this section is being read by the parents or someone elder in the family for looking for guidance for a teen age folks. Please do recommend them reading this section and the book.

Don't overload them with mountainous expectations: It is the responsibility of the parents (or guardians) not to load these teens with mountainous expectations. Many parents want to fulfill their own desires through their child. By all means do suggest the advantages and disadvantages of the career options, jobs etc., but don't push them to the brink. Remember every child is unique and has its own destiny; we need to just allow him/her to blossom. Don't replace your lack of attention or time by splurging on material goodies. Expose them with suitable spiritual literature and let them see the larger purpose of life which has career, wealth, self-realisation and service to others.

Pick up at least one life long hobby: I strongly encourage all of you including young teenagers to pursue one good hobby. This should be creative one and not picked up for the sake of making money or whiling away your time. Making a choice of field of study should be based on your inner desire and interest rather than what is in demand in the market. As by the time you would graduate the world will change and something else will be in demand.

Pray often: You must set aside some time for prayer especially to the Goddess of learning to give you the right wisdom. Either soon after getting up or after taking bath set aside few minutes, recite few verses/ shlokas

/ shabd or any other hymn and light a incandescent stick or candle.

Take care of house chores: You must participate in the house hold activity, however insignificant it may be. Spending some time with elders and seeking some inputs from time to time will help. If you do not do well in an exam or two do not get disappointed, just try harder next time.

Do one thing at a time: Develop focus in whatever you do. If you are playing, just play. If you are studying don't do it in front of the television.

Lead younger folks: Play with younger siblings and try to act a role model for them. Don't compete too much with everyone. The world has place for everyone.

Twinkling Twenties: You may have just crossed the first mile stone of your life. The degree or diploma may be in hand or in the close sight. Given the economic boom all around one job or the other should not be problem for most of you. So the first attempt should be to make yourself productive. Focus on Artha factor at this stage. You are at the most productive part of your life hence the duty or Karma would be the next one to consider.

But you may be confused a bit at this phase of your life. This is not unusual every one of us have been in similar predicament during these years of our life. Perhaps a better job in a different city or country was your choice that has not materialised. The salary may be less as compared to your friends or worst still you may have all the above but nothing useful and worth while to do.

The later may happen if you have joined a big organisation that has too many people like yourself so you have to compete with others to find a right role.

The role may be alluding to you because your lack experience etc.

This is the right time to start firming up your Work life Balance vision.

Balance your vision on your life's objective. Look at the factors those are most important for you that the job offers. Look at the company, role, salary and place of work and see which one are more important than others and take decision accordingly.

Let us stay temperamentally you are an entrepreneur and want to do things of your our choice. Entrepreneurs take initiatives for running things that they are passionate about. Yet you lack money or business acumen to start your own business. So what do you do? Don't jump a stable job next day, wait till you get some more sense of how business is run, gather more industry experience, detail out your business plan, talk to friends and form a team, and then only branch out.

I know of a bright student with research bent of mind who refused to take up an investment banking job and preferred to work with research organisation. In few years time he was a recipient of President's young scientist award. He may have compromised a bit on his remuneration but he could balance stability with achievements very well. Another bright girl preferred not to join IT biggies in an alien city, working on narrow repeated tasks that these companies offer to a fresher. She also disliked living in PG accommodation and surviving eating fast food. She opted to the surprise of many, a role in a large PSU that gave here job variety, more opportunities for people interaction. She got posting in her home city was an added attraction.

Keep focus to give some time to yourself: Remember, at

this stage onwards you should not get pushed by what others are achieving. It is like driving on the street. Don't get discouraged, induced or excited by others choice, keep focus on your vehicle and its steering, your life.

Choose companion wisely: This is also a time when you will be looking for a life partner. In the current context this area is a major concern for many. Look for a partner with a view of what you can add value to him or her, not the other way. Of course he or she should be deserving of your companionship, compatible with your value system, back ground etc., and should ring the bell, as they say in romantic novels. Beware of self-centered, too demanding, possessive variety who wants to be one up every where. Don't get swayed by the movie stories of extreme attractions as their longevity is a suspect. Here too look for the complete package not just one or two features. Be confident with your choice but do discuss with your well wishers. I guess parents still fall under this category!

Thriving Thirties: I get most cases of work like balance problems from this segment. Many of them are due to the earlier decision as well as present indecision. If you don't choose the job that is in commensurate with your life aspirations, you will regret it. Most traveling jobs come very heavy on the family life and health. The novelty of visiting places and flying at 30000 ft height twice a week wears off soon.

There is another problem that plagues this age group which is simultaneously managing family responsibilities as well as career which seem to be at a stage of taking off. As the family making continues the child arrives. Both working partners start having a fight on responsibility sharing of house hold chores, finances or of the child. Both have their career priorities which need to be compromised to attend to child when sick, or dropping it to the school etc.

The principle of WLB remains the same. Start with the key questions what you want to achieve in life, what are the priorities etc. And of course balance your priorities amongst artha, dharma, kama, mokshya factors and draw a plan for next 5 years, together. For example if you feel the career is the priority for next 5 years for both of you, be prepared to be a weekend spouse or living life like a virtual family, ensure that no child to joins you. Yet if you have chosen it otherwise be ready to sacrifice some of your career ambition following the 'give back theory' of mokshya and do not expect that only your spouse should do the same.

Be ruthlessly efficient with your time: Be efficient to save time in daily chores. This will give you more time to devote to the family responsibility.

Use FLIP model: Prioritise your home related work also using this model

Depend on the family support system: There is no need to be rebellious or off-beat to bear the burden of skewed work life challenges. Be gracious to accept your folly and reach out to your family support system as necessary.

Use technology to the maximum: Many organisations allow tele-working, remote working and allow employees to work from home. Utilise every such feature that is available for use. Similarly you can use technology gadgets to keep at tab of children at home when you are at work.

Use organisation flexibility: Choosing the organisation that gives flexibility and WLB feature is a key step. Till the time WLB becomes a prevalent practice, at least one of the partners must consciously choose a company/profession that facilitates this.

Remember you are doing a God's job to take care of your own children the way our parents did for us. Without a bit of sacrifice from both the parents the life of the child would never shape up.

Mid career: These are the years when the WLB is the worst affected. Remember the balancing four factors are equally true at this stage too. Don't over do in any one of them. If the work front is stable put some focus on your family. If the personal front is reasonably under control take a change of career in the right direction that you always lounged for. Or go on a sabbatical to rejuvenate your learning to get a degree that can help you in the long term. This is also a time to plan for the next phase of your life, that is, retirement.

Matured career: You may be at a stage when the past successes or failures would be either enchanting you or haunting you. In either case you will be in a perplexed situation and likely to adopt an attitude of non-action.

Forget the past whatever it was, whether good or bad, and take a renewed pledge to chart out a new course. Make sure the missing excitement of the life is brought back through a balanced approach. Take a resolve that you will reinvent your life at this crucial mid life stage.

This is also the time to re explore your financial capabilities one more time, take initiatives that can help you get a decent post retirement occupation. Many entrepreneurs have come up during this stage of their life when their responsibilities were over yet the desire existed to do something different. Take risk but with caution, don't play gamble.

This is also the time to slow down, look for the larger meaning of life and increasingly spend time on 'mokhsya' pursuit, giving back to society or engaged in philanthropic activities.

Retried or semi-retired: Don't be afraid that the life is in the last leg therefore there is nothing further to look up to. Look around and you will find a number of great achievers have matured in this stage. Many choose to devote time in community service and social cause to their utmost satisfaction. Resolve that every day of your life would be worth adding value to the people around you.

Face the life by making it more useful to the people around you by doing significant duty. Maintain your finances prudently so that you don't have to depend on someone else. Also catch up with all the learning, spiritual activities and hobbies.

Figure 5.3 gives a pictorial representation of what effort-mix can be adopted at different stages of our life.

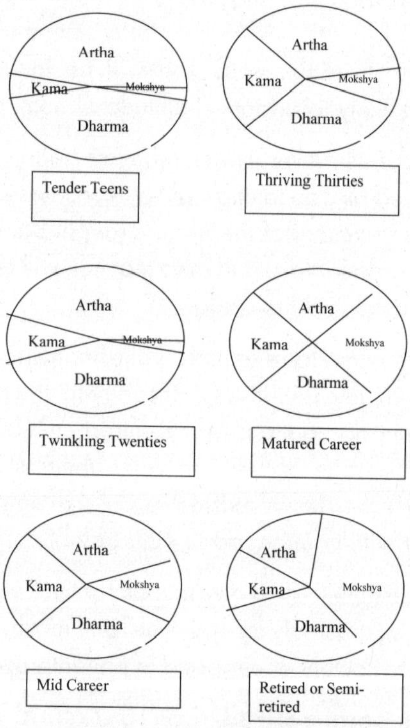

Figure 5.3: Suggested focus of work life balance at different stages of life

Yet Never Clinch on to the present for too long

> *You must know when to leave a place even if you don't have a place to go*
>
> —Anonymous

Monkey catchers adopt a simple technique to catch monkeys. They usually bury an earthen bowl with narrow neck and place some peanuts inside. The monkeys put their hands inside and clench their fists to grab peanuts but are not able to take it out with the grabbed peanuts through narrow neck. They thus get firmly trapped. If they could let go the peanuts they could get themselves free but their inability to let the peanut go, traps them forever. Similarly we all must 'let go' our old attachments if we want to set ourselves free from the earlier stages to move to the next stage.

It is most difficult to let go something that seems to be in hand, today and is real. This happens to most of us. We would like to hold on to a job, role or business even if it is in the decline path. There is no-burning platform desire to jump out to try something else and make a choice between certain death and possible death.[5] It is most tricky when to decide to move on in such situations. Some have done it very successfully and surprised everyone.

It is no wonder when a highly successful chairman of a telecom major decides to turn venture capitalist or a senior executive of a successful MNC starts to work in the social sector they simply uphold their desire do something new and do not want to clinch on to their present. But for such people, a next generation enterprise, successful team or new ventures would not have seen the light of the day and these people would have remained insatiate with their inner desire. What does a successful mountaineer do when he scales one peak; he simply starts all over again at the foot hills of another!

[5]The burning platform syndrome is called for a situation when few people jump from a burning oil drilling platform in the cold and hostile sea to make a choice between 'sure death' as the platform is burning or 'possible death' where they try to save their life by swimming to the shore. Both choices are difficult to say the least. Yet, in management literature, this syndrome is used to provoke people to take action in a declining situation.

Let us contain our desires

Now you must be thinking how can it be? A life without desire is not for ordinary human beings and perhaps reserved for saints and those who have renounced the world. Such people are non-existent in current times. Remember, I am only recommending removing those desires that have no end. Somewhere we must realise that all business enterprises will not be the biggest and only few of us will get the top job or superstar status. I am only suggesting to you to remove this 'top job' clutter from your mind and you will find that you days are much better and balanced. In fact, many of us will be surprised to know that without aggressively courting such desires and scheming about, it may land up on your lap by a stroke of destiny. Any person who does his best in whatever role is given to him is sure to get a better one next time as destiny brings unforeseen opportunities to such persons. Accept the reality that many things in life need not be desired however coveted they may be. Leave it to destiny and good work; they will come to you sooner or later or maybe never. How does it matter?

All desires must have an expiry date

There is another challenge when we continue to hold our desires well past their time. We must know till when to desire for what. If the time to realise these desires has gone by, let us not try to live in the past. I am reminded of two lines from a Hindi film song which say:

> जिंदगी के सफ़र में गुजर जाते हैं जो मक़ाम वो फिर नहीं आते
> *Jindagi ke Safar mein guzar jate hain jo makam, who phir nahi aate.*[6]

Though in the original film the hero wanted to win back his long lost love after several years, I find these two lines very apt in work situations as well. Call it the 'prime ministerial desire syndrome', which most

[6]Those milestones that pass by on the life path don't come back. A song from the Movie *Aap ki Kasam ….. ek baar chale jaate hai jo din raat subaah shaam, woh phir nahi aate*…translated it means those mornings and evenings that pass away never return. Poet Anand Bakshi Ed: Translation of the highlighted text not provided

ageing Indian politicians hold to aspire for the coveted chair throughout their life time. It was truly wise for Sachin to follow a different path and withdraw from the race of captaincy and focus on his game.

Once a senior of mine left his coveted position in a huff and resigned. But he soon intensified his repeated try to come back to the same organisation for the same or higher position. He continued to send feelers through several emissaries to the senior management to reconsider his return. In addition he kept checking with ex-colleagues about what was going on and how the new 'guy' was doing. Perhaps he even thought that if the new guy failed to perform, he may be recalled. Jeeva recalled the sentence he read some where that 'you must burn the bridges behind' whenever he had took up a new job or assignment. Jeeva always made sure not to continue his interest with his ex-department or organisation as soon as he moved on, barring social and personal matters. Not as an act of arrogance but just to not remain hooked on to his past.

All these people desiring to clinch on to their past are simply are wasting their time. Ironically this phenomenon is not specific to any age group. Numerous stories of spurned lovers becoming aggressive criminals, revengeful to an extent of either killing the ex- or themselves appear in newspapers almost every day. There has to be a time and place to let go of a desire and move on. The life will give us new love, new beloved and new opportunities.

Our age old Indian wisdom suggests renunciations of desires as one of the means leading to self-actualisation. The concept of observing fast, ignoring salt or sugar on certain days of the week, helps us control our desire of excesses. Many religions consider fasting as one of the means to express self control and abstaining from carnal desires. Ramdan, the holy month is observed every lunar year where Muslims all over the world fast during the day time for the entire month[7]. In Christianity fasting is considered a self-sacrifice that makes

[7]In Islam, the fast of Ramadan is not just a ritualistic, ceremonial period during which the Qur'an was revealed to the Prophet as a code of conduct and the means of salvation. Fasting the month of Ramadan is a major discipline on the road of personal spiritual transformation. Source: http://www.arclondon.org/fasting-an-overview/ Accessed 27032014.

one humble and more accepting of God's will[8]. As we traverse our life's journey we should increasingly adopt renunciation of desire and prepare ourselves for the day of reckoning.[9]

Be lean, Green and supreme

The work place of today and tomorrow are going to be amorphous and fluid in composition. Not only the team composition changes but the location, logo of the firm, objectives as well as Goals changes dynamically. Most organisation work from quarter to quarter focus, most have their life time of one year after which no one knows what is in store. Such dynamic changes would bring lot of stress to the individual and one may be perpetually in 'proving himself' mode. We cannot change the changes that will come our way but we can glide trough it and negotiate our way around them.

A safe way of driving on a hilly track is to ensure that the vehicle stays within the yellow mark, maintains suggested speed, and the driver keeps a watch on the in-coming vehicles. One also must negotiate bends as they appear on the way. Similarly in our life as well, one needs to constantly follow disciplined path, negotiating the curves but not confronting the obstacles but going around them.

In work situation too the principle of being 'lean' applies almost exactly. Doing your task without creating a fuss, making less demand and throwing no tantrum helps. Becoming efficient and quick to finish the task was another manifestation of being lean. He recalled one of his senior colleague calling himself a 'low maintenance' guy, meaning he does not need too many secretaries, large office space or waiting cars for him to pick up. Being lean not only creates a good vibes with the colleagues but also makes one more useful to the organisation.

The second principle Jeeva adopted was to be a 'green' employee. Green is a principle adopted for equipments and processes that create

[8]Moses fasted for forty days in preparation for receiving the Ten Commandments (Exodus 34:28) Source: http://www.christianbiblereference.org/faq_fasting.htm Accessed 27032014.

[9]In the Bible, the day of reckoning is the day at the end of the world when God will judge everyone.

less pollution in the environment. It is rather strange that polluting vehicles are used, giving great comfort to the people sitting inside but leave a great discomfort to the people on the way side. Similarly, applying this principle for work behaviour means that one should attain progress in his career but not by demeaning others or spoiling the organisation climate. We have already talked about being less-bitching, less-whining while at work. Leaving a sense of positivity while you work with others will earn you respect of the fellow professional. People conceal information, hesitate to share the tip or two with colleague and don't warn them of the impending danger of task, with hope that the other guy will get troubled and the perpetrators derive pleasure out of it.

Jeeva started to extend his helping hand to colleagues even though it may not be asked or entrusted to him as a responsibility. He decided to reach out to people in case it helps them with his advice. Most lateral joiners find the new organisation sometimes confusing, threatening or complex to manage. Jeeva would reach out with his counsel from time to time and help them settle down. Similarly the younger folks in the organisation are always bewildered, lost or feel directionless, Jeeva would become their informal mentor to give an advice or two in their career track or just solving a transactional problem. For Jeeva a tree is unique example that helps the civilisation through its shade, wood, fruit leaves and of course life giving oxygen. In the similar way a green employee will not only produce the results expected of him but also be useful for others even though there is no apparent reason for him to be so. But tree remains static despite the fact they give so many things and grow over a period of time! For Jeeva was convinced that it better to be a static tree giving fruits and shades to others than be a rolling stone that does not gather mass.

The last on his list was to be *supreme*. He did not want to be supreme in terms of rank or authority but in terms of quality. Most people do (or strive to do) a good job only when the task is high profile and under the management's watch. Many don't want to touch what is called a 'donkeys' job from a barge pole. Jeeva observed the attending nurses who irrespective of the nature of task or the patient; performed their job with equal precision and interest. Similarly he decided that now onwards he would strive with similar consciousness of quality as he would do for a high profile task. 'If the task is given to clean the floor he would clean as such that people can see their reflection', he remembered one of his colleague once saying so. He accepted many such assignments which others found too 'messy' of 'low profile' and proved that there is no dearth of making qualitative and quantitative improvements in any task howsoever routine and down under it may be.

The approach helped him to find more satisfaction with his work, more peace in his mind and create better conducive environment at work place. Growth in career was now a just matter of natural progression about which he was neither getting impatient nor concerned.

Focus on immediate work not on results

Remember a saying:

> समय से पहले और किस्मत से ज्यादा कभी किसी को नहीं मिलता
> *Which means that before time or more than the destiny one would never achieve anything.*

From the work life balance perspective,this belief does not mean one should be fatalistic but it only means that one should not worry too much about the results and loose his/her cool but focus on the task at hand and doing it with utmost sincerity and with quality. A widely quoted shloka of *Gita* also says:[10]

> कर्मण्ये वाधिकारस्ते म फलेषु कदाचना
> कर्मफलेहतुर भुरमा ते संगोस्त्वकर्मानी॥ च २, ४७

Ironically, Jeeva in the past had never understood the true meaning of this sholka and at times, like many people with 'new found wisdom',

[10]*Karmanye vadhikaraste ma phaleshu kadachna, Karmaphalehtur bhurma te sangostvakarmani.* Ch. 2, 47 Meaning You have a right to perform your duties but have no control over its results.

was a critic of this thought relegating such thoughts to be meant for losers or failed personalities who needed some excuse to hide. He now understood that results are not only in the form of material or monetary reward we often alluded to, and get disappointed if we don't get the desired credits. The soldiers who fight brilliantly but are not able to capture the enemy post are equally brave. Their sacrifices are no less than soldiers who would have won the battle. The project manager who misses the deadline just because a shipment does not arrive on time despite his painstaking follow-up must memorize this shloka to maintain their composure. Now Jeeva realised the meaning of 'selfless' karma from the work life perspective. It would have been good if you get the results of your efforts but if you don't then never get disappointed and loose your heart.

Doing the job well is far greater satisfaction than the credit it brings.

But be cautious of the time at your disposal

Life for most of us passes in fast forward mode especially when the going is good and it fun all around. But one must be cautious if he is charting every day in the right direction or not as the time will soon run out and one would find himself in situation which is aptly described by the Hindi poetry by Kabir:

तूने रात गवाई सोई के दिवस गवाई खाई
हीरा जनम अमोल था कौड़ी बदले जाई .... कबीर

Raat gawai soye ke, divas gawaya khaye ke;
Hire jaisa janm hai, kaudi badle jaye[11]

And then it will lead to what noted poet Gopal Das 'Neeraj' has written.

[11]Translated it means ... You sent your nights while sleeping and day for eating and in the process wasted your diamond like life in lieu of copper.

Neend bhi khuli na thi ki hai dhoop dhal gayi,
Paon jab talak uthe ki zindagi fisal gayi,[12]

नींद भी खुली न थी की हाय धूप ढल गयी
पाँव जब तलक उठे की जिंदगी फिसल गयी .... गोपाल दास नीरज

Not doing right things at the right time will lead to lot of disappointment and then it would be too late to recover the lost time. This is a dangerous situation if we are putting our life on a rudderless boat and with no destination in our thoughts, sailing to nowhere. The time is short and we must make most of it.

As Swami Vivekanand's says *Arise awake and stop not till the goal is reached,* I urge you all to strive for the Work life balance as the time is running out in our life every day.

Summary of key themes

1. Life is defined to pass through four stages,
   a. Student,
   b. Householder,
   c. Hermitage, and
   d. Renunciation.
2. One must behave appropriately at each of these stages.
3. Follow the 'I' metaphor for managing the life stages'
4. Take steps to renew your career continuously.
5. Life a series of 'S' curves; start the next phase much before the earlier phase is over.
6. Control your insatiable desires.
7. Different stages of life need different approaches.
8. Be lean, green and supreme in terms of the quality of your work.
9. Focus on work, but don't get disappointed when you don't get commensurate results
10. Time is short; take proactive steps to utilize your time in the best ways possible.

[12]Translated it means.... By the time I got up sun was already about to set, by the time I started to step out the life has already slipped by.

CHAPTER SIX

Managing Peaks and TROUGHS

'If you want the rainbow you've got to put up with the rain'. ...

—Dolly Parton[1]

It is part of our life: Let me assure you that no life howsoever endowed and well-inherited it may be, however high and mighty it may belong to, will see only ups, ups and ups! There will be days and years of low, which all of us have to go through.

Don't just look at today's celebrities who currently hog the breaking news arena at every move of their personal life. Either in the past or in the future, they have had or will have their share of down under. The newsmakers of yesterdays do have a share of their trough, but that makes just short news limited to 2 centimeter columns.

Traditional wisdom says that what goes up will come down; life cannot be a bed of roses and will have its share of thorns as well. The key is to mange both of them with equal alacrity, patience as well as poise.

This chapter is about how to manage these two extreme situation that we often encounter in our life when we feel everything is great and

[1]Dolly Rebecca Parton (born January 19, 1946) is an American singer-songwriter, author, multi-instrumentalist, actress and philanthropist, best-known for her work in country music.

also when nothing seems to work. It is the later which hurts people the most but if the former is not managed properly the celebrations become short-lived and sadness descends.

Be Sthitaprajna: I advocate my readers to try and adopt the posture of being calm and balanced even during the periods of high as well as lows when it comes in our life and they will. In the *Bhagwad Gita*, Lord Srikrishnan advises his disciple Arjun to become '*sthitaprajna.*'[2] It is attributed to a person who is free from the conflicts of the pairs of opposites, such as pain and pleasure, virtue and vice, honour and dishonour, and good and evil. In short, *sthitaprajna* means being free from all attachments and aversions. A balanced individual will have to put through his lows and troughs as carefully as he has to manage his peak and glory.

Such a person is not very elated when he achieves something spectacular. He never starts going about town to narrate his supernatural prowess. He never claims, 'I am the best', and starts singing and dancing atop his house or on the street as the case may be. The higher the achievement, the lower will be the display of pleasure for such a person.

Remember the modest display of emotions by Dr Abdul Kalam when he was elected the President of the largest democracy of the world. He only made a short thank you speech, that's all.

Dr Kalam is like many of us, a person of humble beginnings, born amongst many siblings to a villager father. He worked his way up to become a scientist by profession. I am sure he would have neither dreamt nor intended to be a public figure, let alone become the President of India. However, when he attained this coveted position that was till then reserved only for seasoned politicians of the ruling combine, few raised their eyebrow for his non-conventional style. To the surprise of many, he proved truly equal if not more, a match to the highest civilian position in this country. People say that he re-wrote the job description of the coveted office that was till then believed as nothing more than ceremonial in nature. He rejuvenated the role of a President in twenty-first century India

[2]*Gita*, The verses 55 to 72 in Chapter 2 discusses the virtues of Sthitaprajna in greater details.

by actively prompting to take steps to bring knowledge economy culture, establishing communication with the people, especially with young students who just loved his unconventional style. When he demitted this office, he went back to teaching and living like any other common citizen.

On the contrary, you would have seen the pomp and show created by some up-start politicians who just win their first local municipal elections. They lead a pompous procession while standing atop an open truck with an accompanying music band and slogan-shouting followers. These individuals after having lost their next elections never forget to mention their 'former' status in every letter they write and throw their weight around on people they come in contact with. Neither in peak nor in trough are they able to balance themselves.

Have you ever seen Sachin Tendulkar dancing after finishing any of his milestones of records? However, vivid images of exuberance by some of the one-match wonders are galore

Peaks and troughs—it will happen to us. We only need to manage them well. Unfortunately competitive situations of the current world do force us to visualise only success. How foolish and yet strange to always believe that I will win!

We are told that unless we visualise success and consequently aim for it, we will not get it. But, can someone ensure that I will succeed in every job interview, every relationship, and all types of investments, despite these visualisation? What do I do when I fail?

Just wait for your time to come

No one tells us how to deal with rejection, failure and disappointment. Let me add few suggestions to you on how to deal with such situations. First of all take it lightly, under play it, thank the almighty that the failure could have been worse and be confident on your ability to succeed as always. Just behave in a similar fashion as if you have succeeded!

Don't cry your heart out, blame the judges of the competition where you were participating, go into depression and take recourse to drug, despair or death. So what if you have failed in one exam or denied one salary increase? Even failure in love, let's say when the other guy (or gal) is not in agreement to continue, the entire world has not depleted of human beings? Is it necessary just because of one failure, you have to take life of yours, his, hers or their parents that we see in news every other day. Don't fix the blame on someone (including you) and go after it to revenge. Failure and success are the two sides of the same coin that is called life.

Just move on after every such situation. Life is a beautiful present from God through our parents; we have to take it through a roller coaster ride as it unfolds. One or two rejections at regular intervals are just fine!

In earlier pages we have talked about the responsibility of results is not in our hands. This does not mean that we should not put in enough efforts just because results are unpredictable. Not all plants bear fruits every season yet the gardener tile and water them every day.

My father was once very upset sitting reminiscing about a major theft in the house. He had practically lost everything, Being in the law enforcement services he often had to face threat form disgruntled criminals against whom he would have acted tough in the past. Clearly this act was well-planned and well-executed by someone with great grudge, otherwise it would not have been possible to enact such a cleanup act with armed guards and hordes of staff present in his bungalow on the fateful night.

Then one afternoon his close friend arrived and asked a simple question.

'Looks like this is an act by someone who wanted to settle a score with you?'

My father nodded as he was worried as to how will he resurrect his savings and get back jewellery that my mother had lost.

His friend patted my father's back and said 'You should be happy as those guys only took away your wealth which you can earn in due course. What if those guys harmed you or your family?

My father got the answer to manage his trough. He realised that now onwards he would focus on the silver linings in every cloud. He would not loose his sleep for lost days, money or position. My father would repeat this story to all of us when we used to hit a low in our life, be it in exams or play. Even if any of our siblings obtained low grades in any examination, he would simply say 'nothing to worry now prepare for the next one'. I am sure that modern parents need a lesson or two when they get worried about a few percentage points of their child and sometimes drive their children crazy when they do not score adequately.

In a career span of 30–40 years there will be some days, some weeks, months or years that will be good and some will certainly not be so good. Like stock market indices, it will have its peaks and troughs. Seasoned stock brokers in who deal with stock market advice to be cautious in investing in those stocks that are too volatile and trading at all time high prices, as the fall may be imminent and therefore a huge loss lurking behind the corner. Similarly when the prices are low they would advice to be prudent with few stocks that have good fundamentals not on those which seems to be just on low on prices.

So when you get the good raise in you career, go slow, give yourself time to settle down and savour the pleasure of reaching the peak.

Likewise when you face dejection, make more efforts to stay put. Take your next steps cautiously and 'buy' as your friendly stock broker would have advised when the chips are down, some more time. This is not to say that one should become insensitive to the pain of failure or should not enjoy pleasure, but try to transcend them. Accept both pain and pleasure. Don't hide your failures and take full responsibility for them; only then the pain will go away. Failure or success has to be accepted with grace and humility.

Osho says that if someone experiences happiness fully, if he is utterly sensitive to pleasure, if he lives it so totally that nothing remains to be lived, he will soon transcend it. Then he will be unperturbed and steady in every situation of pleasure and happiness. Similarly if someone experiences pain and misery totally, if he goes into it with all his being, without trying to escape it in the least, he too will go beyond pain; he will never again be disturbed by suffering. Krishna does not ask you to kill your sensitivity; on the contrary, he wants you to heighten your sensitivity to its utmost, so it becomes total.

In fact, seasoned coaches tell their players to *give their best while playing and worry least about the results.* When the team wins, the seasoned managers and coaches want the team to take it easy and not let their success get into their heads. Similarly, when the team looses a match they make sure the team just returns to practice sessions the very next day. It was feat to watch the emotional display of Argentina's coach Diego Armando Maradona after the crushing defeat of his team by Germany during the 2010 Fifa world cup. He was just hugging and kissing each player as if telling them 'manage your trough guys. Manage it'

Similarly in our career there will be situations of highs and lows. Just take them in your stride and wait for the next opportunity.

How to overcome the trough?

When you hit the valley of despair, at times it looks difficult to manage, but you will, just by taking few simple actions. Eckhart Tolle in his book *Power of Now*[3] says, when you are in truly dump situation you must first accept that you are in mess and accept your responsibility. Once you accept that you are in a mess you will have the courage to accept the situation and forge a way to come out. Never be in the denial mode, blame someone else for your situation (it may be true even though) or wait for someone to rescue you. Accept, take action and move on.

But at the same times I suggest that take it easy as failure is part and parcel of any life's journey. Like success, failure is also transient in nature.

All the super achievers who play a long innings or have a career spanning many decades show high energy and seem impervious of such high and lows. They accept that trough will soon pass as the night passes to usher a sunlit day. One needs to rest, rejuvenate and prepare for the next day during the trough when another peak would invite him to its fold. One of the ways to manage a low is have lower expectation after every high result. Try this out it really works!

[3]The Power of Now: A Guide to Spiritual Enlightenment by Eckhart Tolle Publisher: New World Library; 1ST edition (August 19, 2004) ISBN-10: 1577314808 ISBN-13: 978-1577314806.

Take the case of Eisenstein who obtained poor grades in his schools but went on to be the greatest scientist of his times. Edison, the famous inventor has a beautiful advice for people who get discouraged by failures. He said he got his famous light bulb glowing only after witnessing a series of failures. When he was asked about his failure, he replied that these were not the failures his discovery of a 100 different ways why the light bulb will not work!

Plan for the next steps, gather the courage and time it to take action. Never get too pleased or too depressed; time is transient and will change, sooner than expected.

I am bemused with the statistics of what success does when tasted early in life. Several of our friends and colleagues, celebrities included, just falter after huge first time success. To me it is not their inability to manage their success the first time but the subsequent lows soon after. Once you achieve a peak, super success such as topping the coveted civil services exams or delivering a hit movie, the next day becomes difficult to live by. You may be confused if the success was due to your hard work, luck or just being at the right place at the right time. So reinitiating yet another grueling effort for the next climb may be too much for you. You may tend to bask in its glory become used too and relax a bit. The next achievement may not be as good, your next movie may bomb on the box office or you may be out on the first ball itself. This failure comes as rude shock, 'how can it be to me?' and people start talking around that 'he is no good'. Your life then drifts itself into depression. Like failure, consider the huge success as something of past and move on with renewed zeal and preparedness for the next task. A famous celebrity star has commented once that he treats every movie like his first movie and wherever he has taken it lightly, the success has eluded him. Sooner you throw off the past baggage of either success or failure, better it will be.

Once in my life I had to take a rather unusual decision. Leaving a high sounding, high profile position, I had to take up a rather obscure role to lead a start-up venture. The role model to such career change are the mountaineers who after scaling a mighty peak, also successfully and safely climb down from and prepare themselves to scale the new ones in the next season, may not be as high.

Seek help if required

Never be shy to seek help in case you need in these situations from people whom you trust. Beware of the people who are fair whether friends and there are many every where.

Unless you reach out for help many of your true friends would not know. In such cases, you can decide the quantum of help required and the tone of communication to adopt. Neither sending mass mailers will help nor knocking the doors of close friend at the dead of the night will. Be careful about the choice of person and words while seeking help. Ask for advice that most people would be willing to. Yet don't expect everyone will keep running with open arms and lift you on their shoulders. There would be constraints and limitation for everyone. Finally only at a last resort ask for financial help, which may not come and you may loose a supporter in the bargain.

For seeking help you must look helpless. Most people brag what they have and how influential they are and then ask for help as if they are doing a favour. Help can come from a smallest person or from someone totally unknown. Remember you take shelter under the tree someone else has planted. Be grateful to the person and God almighty for having connected you with that person who came forward for help.

बड़े प्यार से मिलना सब से दुनिया में इन्सान से,
क्या जाने किस भेस में बाबा मिल जाएँ भगवान रे[4]

Story: I should have shared my problems

Viru[5] called Jeeva after nearly 10 years. During this period all efforts to locate him had proved futile. Viru

[4]'Bade Pyar Se Milna Sabse'. Film Name: Sati Ansuya. Year: 1956 Lyrics Pt. Roopnauth Sharma. Translated it means … Meet with every one with love and affection as on never knows when he will meet God.

[5]Not of *Sholey* fame.

had not left any address, mobile number or email id to reach him at.

'Where did you disappear, my friend?' was a natural question posed to him by Jeeva.

'We must meet before you go away,' Jeeva insisted.

He was one of the chosen colleges and batch mate who was destined to do well in his life. He was a good student, a committed professional and lovable friend who could do no wrong in was everyone's belief. Predictably his growth was fast and he soon occupied a leadership role in his mid-career years. He was one such person who receives his peers' admiration as well as jealousy. Yet, for such a person a sudden disappearance was surprising.

'I had to leave the high profile job in a huff. The promoters had embezzled financial institution funds into their personal kitty and tax authorities were knocking my door as I was a signatory to most of the document as the CEO'. He sipped tea after taking a bite from a steaming hot samosa. Then he added, 'I just went underwater. I joined 3 positions below in another company at lower salary and of course, far less associated perks. I was afraid to share my problem with any one'.

'But you should have called me. As a friend I had every right to be a part of your troubled days like we were in good old days' Jeeva said.

Jeeva thereafter went off to explain his new found philosophy of his work life balance after his recent accident.

'I was very focused on my career and look at where I am? I still haven completed my family responsibilities'. His friend ruefully said,

'But you are alive and your life is not yet over. Remember what Rahim said,

रहमिन चुप हो बैठयि देख दनिन के फेर जब नीके दनि आएंगे बनत न लगहि देर',[6] Jeeva added.

The evening stretched till wee hours sharing the amazing insights about people and times during this period. Both friends were able to rescue each other from depressing thoughts that one gets into under these circumstances. They realised that these events, though of different nature, had made them stronger and wise.

'I think I should have talked to you long back.' said an SMS few days later from Viru.

Manage peaks with more caution: Managing success is difficult than managing failure. Remember driving down hill on a traffic free hilly road is a temptation. Most drivers press the gas more and catch up with speed. This is act leads them to throw caution to winds and loose control of the vehicle. No one knows what is lurking at the next bend or next curve and then the accident happens. Seasoned driver on hilly track become cautious when driving down hill. Such drivers choose more often the break than accelerator.

When you are doing well, perched on the top of the world, be careful while exercising power or taking liberty with finances or people. Consider all the risk for getting associated with ventures and organisers who may have dubious track record. Many leading executives and leaders have invited extreme rebuttal from the law and corporate board when they were found wanting while socialising or with their expense account.[7] In the hindsight these errors would

[6]*Rahiman chup ho baithiye dekh dinan ke pher, jab neeke din ayenge banat na lagihe der*... Translated it means ... Rahim, keep quite and watch the turn of events, when the good days will arrive things will change very fast Abdur Rahim KhanKhana (also known as Rahim),who lived during the reign of Akbar. This couplet says that one should wait for the times to change, which will happen sooner than expected.

[7]The Economic Times, 13th August 2010, 'Hurd Mentality: Why big minds trip over small things'. Available at http://economictimes.indiatimes.com/news/news-by-industry/et-cetera/Hurd-Mentality-Why-big-minds-trip-over-small-things/articleshow/6302724.cms.

look foolish and unbelievable that it was such high profile and widely acknowledged people would have made such indiscretions. Some of them were careless, some arrogant, some so sure of themselves that it did not bother to check. Some who thought they have now 'arrived' hence these minor transgressions would not matter at all. But it did and they finally lost their job, went to grueling days of bad publicity and of course paid hefty 'out of court settlements' just wriggle themselves out. In the days of spy cams, byte hungry TV channels and perfect traceability through call-records and email trails, the only way one can manage falling in a trap or not being caught after making a mistake is keep him / her squeakily clean, preserved and pure. Caution is the best policy for survival when you are in command and seemingly perched on top.

Be extra cautious of your choice of words, actions or friends during highly successful phases. Be wary of hanger-on's or falling at your feet admirers during those good run of your life. Your true friends and well wishers will be shy to meet you and if they do they would suggest you to take achievements easy as if nothing has happened to you. Your true admirers would not create scenes by shouting slogans from the roof tops in your favour. Be humble in receiving praise, leave arrogance for some other day and manage your time well for the next step of your life, which no one knows what it will bring.

Diversify your interests: The high and low cycle is applicable to fresh graduate or an experienced professional equally. Experts advice that during the cycles of low gather more positives than negatives, use the time to develop new skills, diversify, develop new talent, attend new courses or just study at home. The trough of time, ironically may not be your making, this could be due to now the infamous sub-prime crisis, change of management or mergers and acquisition or what ever, that may lead you to loose your job, position or perks. Diversify yourself and seek new avenues, the trough of time will soon pass.

If you follow some of these principles then you will find your life will be in much more balanced form. Try these thoughts, adopt them and also share your experience and results with people around you. Give back your learning's and pleasure of having accomplished work life balance in such situations.

Summary of key themes

1. Life will have uncertainties. There will be high points and low days.
2. One must try to maintain a balance during pain and pleasure, honour and dishonour by becoming a *Sthitaprajna* personality, who is free from all attachments and aversions.
3. A balanced individual will have to put himself through his lows and troughs as carefully as he has to manage his peak and glory.
4. In the case of high points, don't go overboard; control your calm and ego. Act with more humility than you normally do to maintain your composure.
5. In case of low points, accept them as they are, continue to look forward with renewed hope and wait for your time to shine.
6. Maintain low expectations and an alternative fall-back plan in case things don't turn out well.
7. Seek help; we all need it at some point in our life.
8. Yet, don't expect that everyone will help equally; they may have their own limitations or constraints.
9. Manage your peaks with more caution.

Try these thoughts in your own life and share the impact it has made on you.

CHAPTER SEVEN

Aim for Self-ACTUALISATION

What a man can be, he must be. This need we call self-actualization.
—Abraham Maslow

We have discussed various ways in which we can establish work life balance leading to self-paced life that will give us contentment and a sense of control. Such life will also make us more responsible in the larger context of not only our life but towards family, friends and society. Yet the question remains as to what is that unique final point that each one of should strive for. Call it self-actualisation or self-realisation, its meaning however, for common people like most of us, remains to be examined.

Few years later since the unfortunate event Jeeva was sitting in is balcony overlooking the busy traffic laden highway at a distance. He was by then completely recovered both physically and mentally. The recent reassessment of his work life priorities had given him a renewed sense of prioritization of various facades of his life. Family was happy and he was enjoying the bliss of after having come out of a scary situation that has also given him an opportunity to correct himself.

The view from the balcony of his 9th floor apartment was that of a vast track of agricultural land, green and yellow in patches. This was a breathtaking view of greenery split by a 8 lane expressway passing through the middle about a kilometer away from his apartment. This used to present an interesting sight, the unending stream of cars and other vehicles jostling to overtake each other on the expressway and calm and cool agricultural land on ether side with low activity and serenity. His house was equally calm as his wife and children were away to attend a function and he had plenty of time to do nothing. He was happy that he has found ways and means to make his life much more balanced but some times a question kept popping up as what is the purpose and meaning of life? Is it only to be borne, seek pleasure and ultimately die or is it some thing else. He knew that he was not the only one who sought answer to this question but he has to find answer to the meaning and purpose of his life.

19th century's greatest novelists, Leo Tolstoy at the peak of his career and aristocratic life style has similar predicament and devoted several years on this subject to of find the meaning of life[1]. Leo Tolstoy realized that the meaning and purpose of life is more than what the materialistic world thinks. Similarly there are several well known philosophers and thinkers who have devoted time and energy to find answer to this question. Jeeva spent several week skimming through these thinking and came to a conclusion that in plain simple terms life has to have a purpose and meaning which every individual must find and achieve. The birth of a person may be a result of chemical reaction that some of the scientific minds may say but one thing is certain this chemical product has also must find its purpose.

All of us are unique in our own right. We also have a unique capability and purpose for which we have come on this earth. The only challenge is to find these unique capability and the unique purpose and aim to achieve it throughout our life. Most philosophers agree that one of the purpose of the life is to work for humanity and for the service of mankind. Leo Tolstoy surmised several lessons to understand the philosophies of life such as practicing empathy, making a difference to the world we live in, mastering the art of simple living. He also cautioned about our contradictions and

[1]On Life And Essays On Religion (1934) Author: Leo Tolstoy Publisher: Oxford University Press.

struggles one has to face personal transformation as it is easier to say than to practice.

Meaning of Self-actualisation: Noted behavioural scientist Dr Abraham Maslow propagated the term 'self-actualisation'[2] as a man's desire to become what he has the potential and capable of becoming. A self-actualised person will have

- Acceptance and Realistic perceptions of himself and others without any prejudice for others
- Problem solving, helping others approach motivated by a sense of personal responsibility and ethics.
- Spontaneity in thinking and demeanor. It means that he would be open and unconventional yet is not a rebel of sorts and confirm to rules and social expectations.
- Carve for autonomy and solitude. He would like to be with people yet want his own space for developing his own individual potential.
- Willingness to appreciate anything new in the world, however simple it may be to seek source of inspiration and pleasure.
- Ability to attain Peak Experiences[3] such as moments of intense joy, wonder, awe and ecstasy through sheer application of their potential.

The Self-actualisation or fulfillment is the supreme goal of life to be achieved through atma gyanam.[4] Upanishads say a state when you know yourself and you are self-realised. Only those who are pure, free from pride, passion and delusion, who have renounced attachment and constantly dwelling in the Supreme Self, with desires and dualities stilled, can reach the eternal goal (Gita 15.05).[5]

[2]This term was first used in Kurt Goldstein's book The Organism: A Holistic Approach to Biology Derived from Pathological Data in Man Publisher: American Book Company, New York 1939.

[3]Maslow, A. (1970). Motivation and personality (2nd ed.). New York: Harper & Row.

[4]When we look at our thoughts and mind as an outside person or master, we can control our unnecessary thoughts and worries. This is called 'Atma Gnanam' or knowledge of the Atma.

[5]See http://www.happinessoflife.com/.

Self-realisation

All men should strive, to learn before they die,
What they are running from, and to, and why.

—James Thurber

We must have heard the he Ancient Greek phrase 'Know thyself', which has become a synonym for self-realisation or self-knowledge. All Gurus and sage insist that we must know more about ourselves. But this is easier said than done.

Our life is judged so much by others opinion and perceptions that we seldom take our own views seriously. Starting out since our early childhood we see ourselves from others eyes and decide our capabilities and future what other tell us. Many of these opinion makers are true well wishers (such as our parents, friends or family members) whose intentions are noble yet they may not know our hidden potential. This journey of self-actualisation is to unfold our hidden talent and potential which only we as an individual would know.

खुद में खुद को खुद से ही खोजे जाने की
खुद की यह कोशिश बड़ी भली लगती है[6] .... सशंदु

The above means that if we don't strive to search our inner self then we are likely to loose track of the very purpose for which God has sent us for. Living our life without this realisation is like taking a roller coaster ride where there is lot of thrills to experience but without any purpose. Ultimately, such a person just lives for himself, for his sensual gratification and attains nothing personally or spiritually.

The moment we realise and develop deeper understanding of our own self, we will undertake work and vocation that suits our personality. We will then never end up being frustrated in a particular company or job, activities or culture of which does not suit us. We will also not be tempted to take up vocation just because we see others enjoying it but may be totally off our liking.

[6]Translated it means ... Searching self within your own self is welcome attempt.

Greek philosopher Socrates advocated the inner consciousness and advocated that each one of us should be wise to understand his inner voice. If we have not examined ourselves, the unexamined life is not worth living at all. That perhaps is true for most of us. The moment we stop listening to our inner self we end up doing things that we don't like to do. Irrespective of the failure or success of any venture, all that which suits our own liking is far more enjoyable than doing something that is not suited to our personality.

How to lead the self-discovery journey

Nice thought but what next?

This question most of us would have and so did Jeeva when he wanted to take the next step towards self-actualisation. Having crossed several stages that helped him balance his life he, was not yet certain (and he still isn't!) if he was leading the path of self-actualisation.

He vigourously searched material on this subject, searched several sites on the internet and learnt from some of them. There was no 'silver bullet' that he could swallow to follow this path. The Myers-Briggs Type Indicator test, personality type questions, self-help books etc., all added to his knowledge. In fact, he realised that there were several ways through which he could learn himself. While a mirror gives him the body contour and facial expression, the weighing scale gives his weight. These two provide an assessment of two different aspects of his body. Similarly, all these personality tests touch upon few elements of the personality in parts and are never exclusive either / or type tests.

Explore your childhood days

It is said that the uncontaminated child carries the virtues of God. His purity of thoughts and behaviour are the true reflection of the person he would be. Wordsworth (1802)[7] said in one of his famous

[7]"My Heart Leaps Up," William Wordsworth (1770–1850, Cumberland, England).

poems that 'The Child is Father of the Man', meaning that what we think as children will help us determine how we think as adults. The child in every person teaches him to appreciate nature beginning with the simple beauty of rainbows and by implication, other natural wonders which for Wordsworth remained true throughout his life. It is our inner child that will help us point to the great and the wonderful things that we could do in our life.

In addition the way a child is brought up determines what he or she will become in the future. A child's impressionable mind is quick to pick up the good and bad very fast. It is unfortunate that we are subjecting our children with so much of external influence that we are making them loose their innocence too soon. It is like giving hormone injections to ripen tender vegetables which lead to disastrous health consequences.[8]

Jeeva traced his childhood days to explore his inner desires. He used to enjoy making castles and caves on sand beds (like most children do). He would visualise streets, homes and play areas in the city that he would build on the sand bed along with his friends. When he grew up he set up a science lab at home to carry out experiments. He used to develop medicine formulations (some of them backfired when he added wrong portions!) and also churned out home-newspaper everyday carrying news items of family members and visitors. He was bit of a risk taker who will drive his tricycle on the edge of the verandah and hurt himself but the speed was truly enjoying. His lived his life moving from one school to the other. He liked making new friends and also keeping touch the earlier as he moved to new cities due to frequent transfer of his father. He was quick to make friends and adjust in new situations fast enough.

He also recollected what he wanted to become in his childhood dreams. He wanted to be a fighter pilot (may be due to the war hysteria with Pakistan in 19'65 and 1971) and scientist (as he had read the glorious article about Dr Jayant Narliker who with Sir Fred Hoyle synthesized Albert Einstein's Theory of Relativity and Mach's Principle

[8]See 'Indian minister warns of fruit and vegetable hormone injections'. Available at http://timesofindia.indiatimes.com/india/Alarm-over-chemicals-in-veggies/articleshow/6224569.cms.

into conformal gravity theory[9]) and lastly he wanted to sing patriotic songs like Md. Rafi. He had all these traits in demonstrable abilities during his early childhood, many of them fell by the wayside as he grew up and took up only a popular career-oriented approach to his life.

The time had come to 'redeem his pledge', he thought. All the dreams were pointing to him to seek a career laced with creativity, avenues to explore and research with a fair degree of freedom with a sense of patriotism is what his inner self wanted.[10]

Understanding yourself through metaphors

Once Jeeva met a Guru[11] and asked, 'Tell me how do I indentify my hidden talents?' The Guru gave him an amusing look but advised, 'Just identify yourself with one or two metaphors For instance, Jeeva considered himself close to an elephant amongst all animals. He was slow to start but would carry great responsibility (load) and be very useful to his masters and organisation of work. Like an elephant he would remain generally cool and playful. Yet, he was aware of his 'once in a while' elephant-like mad behaviour when pushed to a corner. Such acts he knew were more damaging to him than to others.

Also amongst the mythological characters he felt closer to Hanuman; unpretentious, selfless service, and a no-frill disposition. At the same time Hanuman ji has great wit and ability to innovate and improvise in difficult situations. No wonder his family, friends and office colleague would like to keep him around whenever any problems came up. In fact he would search for such difficult assignments to throw himself in. He liked solving them to get the desired adrenaline rush. Some times he did get hurt in the process, but that is a different

[9]Commonly known as Hoyle–Narlikar theory Ref http://en.wikipedia.org/wiki/Jayant_Narlikar accessed 20032014.

[10]He also remembered his his childhood to understand the weakness of his personality. which helped him to correct himself, for example getting angry easily was one of them that he worked upon.

[11]Mr Rajen Brijnath, Corporate General Manager & Vice-President (Retd.) HR ITC ltd HR Consultant.

discussion. Of course, like Hanuman ji he would also forget easily his own capabilities and needed to be reminded and cajoled by someone.

These two simple steps were good enough for his self-discovery. He shared this simple method of self discovery with his friends and colleagues and many found it very useful. Jeeva, after this became far wiser to refuse assignments and responsibilities that he felt were not creative and problem solving enough giving him ample latitude and freedom to research his own way![12]

Jean Shinoda Bolen,[13] a noted American medical doctor says, 'You have the need and the right to spend part of your life caring for your soul but it is not easy. You have to resist the demands of the work-oriented, often defensive, element in your psyche that measures life only in terms of output—how much you produce—not in terms of the quality of your life experiences. To be a soulful person means to go against the all-pervasive, prove-yourself values of our culture and instead treasure what is unique and internal and valuable in yourself and your own personal evolution.' How true are these words for all of us in our quest of balanced life objectives.

Self-Actualisation is the process to reach that stage when one is able to look for personal evolution of a higher order. Incidentally, this journey is not too difficult to start, Jeeva learnt, tried and received phenomenal returns.

You can do that too.

Summary of key theme

1. Actualisation starts with self-awareness
2. Once you are self-aware, understand your strength and weaknesses, dreams and desires then you can chart out a course of action.
3. Self-actualisation means what one wants to do in his life It also means refusing some things in life that do not suit your inner self.
4. It also means refusing some things in life that do not suit your inner self.

[12]Readers you can also try this Annexure J. Understand yourself though Metaphors in Chapter 11.

[13]www.jeanbolen.com.

CHAPTER EIGHT

Organisation Must ENCOURAGE WLB

There are three stages in a person's life; birth, life and death. They are not conscious of birth, submit to death and forget to live.

—Jean De La Bruyere
(1645–96, French classical writer)

WLB philosophy and the role of organisation

One of the key factors for successful work life balance for any individual is to take up a job in an organisation that supports this philosophy. Some self-employed professions do give better flexibility in this regards than others but also carry risk and uncertainty in the financial front that many may not like to choose. A very large professional workforce is engaged in organised firms where the role of the management is crucial to promote a work life balance (WLB) culture. Ironically, WLB philosophy though gaining ground in private conversation has not got enough mindshare at the level of corporate decision making. For many organisations WLB issues are discussed in soon to be forgotten seminars without any concerted follow through action.

We have argued that it would be naive to assume that work life balance can be achieved through the individual's efforts alone without the support of the organisation. While individuals have to take the lead, it is the organisation that has a decisive role to play. As long as any WLB effort by any individual is looked down upon by colleagues, or managers, considered non-contributing/non-conforming to corporate business objectives, WLB will remain just an empty slogan. In fact, many organisations barring a progressive few, instead of encouraging WLB take the route of retribution. It is no wonder when an article proclaimed that WLB will remain a mere topic of workshop discussion[1] and would never invite serious attention for implementation from the corporations of our times. It is a sad state of affairs but let us see what the firms are going to miss if they do not adopt a WLB philosophy.

Statistics describing current state of affairs: A recent survey[2] shows that while 80 per cent executives opine that work life balance is critical to decide to join or leave a job, yet 82 per cent also say that their company does not have a programme in place to improve work life balance. According to a study conducted by The McCrindle Research[3] with 3000 Australians executives, work life balance is considered as the #1 factor for job attraction and retention (even above the salary). Similar results are also found in other developed countries based out of similar studies. Another research findings shows that 58 per cent of Canadians feel 'role overload'—that is, difficulty in managing different roles in their lives.[4] The same survey also points that 55 per cent of executives surveyed do not have a satisfactory work life balance. With increasing economic pressure

[1]See http://www.thehindu.com/op/2008/01/20/stories/2008012052271400.htm.

[2]The survey was conducted by The Association of Executive Search Consultants (AESC), www.aesc.org and The Economist Intelligence Unit (EIU), www.eiu.com. Available at http://viewswire.eiu.com/report_dl.asp?mode=fi&fi=757215260.PDF.

[3]See www.mccrindle.com.au, and contact mark@mccrindle.com.au for any queries.

[4]A study by Centre for Families, Work and Well-Being at the University of Guelph. Available at www.cmha.ca/data/2/rec_docs/1698_TextofSpeech-final%202008.doc.

on performance, most organisations would resort to overstretching their workforce to do more for less. PricewaterhouseCoopers (PwC), a global management firm, surveyed[5] over 5000 employees in 113 countries to conclude that:

- Employees are more concerned about work life balance.
- 39 per cent people value flexible working arrangements the most encouraging one to select the organisation.
- Flexibility is most sought after in Western Europe and North America.
- A large numbers of respondents hope for a better work life balance in the future.

Indian working class in the last 10–15 years have transformed where both partners in the family work and have a career of their own. Most live away from the joint family system, travel 20–30 kilometers both ways, have kids to look after and have a very busy schedule. No wonder that increased cases of family discord, divorce or separation is seen among young couples in India. 'The nuclear family structure, modern lifestyle and professional tensions may be behind the phenomenal increase in marital discord' quotes a study report.[6] The situation is but the same across cities and economic strata and the cause is also just one—failure to establish the work life balance. These multiple surveys point to just one fact, WLB is a major clamour by executives, yet organisations are doing nothing significant about it.

Multi-tier outsourcing adds to this challenge: The outsourcing phenomenon has given a unique twist to the WLB issue. Employees working for on-site assignments at customer locations have to follow the customer's work timings, use customer premises and facilities, etc. Millions of service industry professionals and workers (blue, white or grey collar) fall under this category. WLB as way of life must be respected by customers, collaborators and others who form the outsourcing work ecosystem. Concerted efforts must be made to undergo cultural and philosophical change by everyone in the service delivery chain.

[5]See http://forums.industryweek.com/showthread.php?t=16081.

[6]See http://www.tribuneindia.com/2007/20070717/main2.htm.

Employers have to help create a responsive culture and environment for WLB

Organisations have to create a receptive cultural environment to respect the personal space of employees and encourage their individual efforts to attain their work life balance. WLB supportive policies coupled with a greater understanding of its underlying principles will go a long way to help establish this approach as best practices for work culture.

We believe that creating a conducive environment to promote work life balance is the sole responsibility of an organisation. It will be hard to aim for work life balance in an organisation where staying past working hours is a norm and taking a genuine leave or vacation is considered a crime. Unfortunately, this culture is no only prevalent in hierarchical or 'mom and pop' firms alone. Some of the new age organisations in the technology sector have also perpetrated WLB imbalance in the garb of 'following-the-sun' working hours, night shifts etc.. Now that we can reach out to employees easily on their mobile phone, email or chats at any time of the day or night, hence we start expecting their presence on a 24×7 basis. In manufacturing organisations, where shift working is a norm, have perfected this art or time rotation and have built adequate safeguards to protect their employees' health. The same is not found in many firms which are in service sector.

WLB culture will benefit organisations immensely: It must be understood that WLB is for the overall benefit of the organisation as much as it is for its employees. Organisations therefore should not shy from adopting this. They have to take similar initiatives as taken in the past for employees' medical insurance, work hygiene and work place safety which were all mandated by law but started off as corporate good practices by progressive companies. Organisations will ultimately find benefit out of a stable workforce such as better quality of work output, better productivity, stability and even fewer cases of emotional disturbances or fraud.

Women employees need to be better supported in this regard than men. Several women who could have had great careers had to cut it short or compromise just because their organisations were not flexible enough to support WLB. If work life balance initiatives are properly implemented in a company, the women employees will get far greater benefits and 68 per cent are likely to reach the top jobs, concluded another survey.[7]

Cultural and Social factors do play a role

The spirit of WLB is also rooted in the country's work culture. Developed countries in the Western world are considered to be more amenable to embrace the WLB philosophy. Asian countries including India and Japan, however, have a different story to tell. In most of these countries work is considered to be the most important activity of an individual's life. Barring few job roles such a teaching or select government jobs, most others suffer from unscheduled work hours, 6 days' work week leading to clocking of 55–60 hours of work a week. Add to this the commute time and intrusion into our personal time through SMS, blackberry and email, the work seems to perpetuate almost round the clock! Now you may turn around and say let us not make WLB as one of the difficult, pervasive, important yet little-actionable problems like environment and ecology. Instead I wish to offer some simple policies that organisations can adopt to see the change in their overall climate. I can assure you of measurable results such as low attrition, and better and quality output.

In South Asian countries, the respect for others' time and space is somewhat compromised. In Western cultures, calling on the cell phone (or home phone) after office hours is strictly no-no and sales calls are limited to only those who have given their consent. The recent telecom boom has led to a mushrooming of call centers, who in order to sell their products tend to disturb us at unwanted hours and even on holidays. We as a society must discourage these people from wasting our time.

Asian countries including India, are known to be on the growth curve of their economies. They have a large pool of high energy young population that needs extra bucks to spend on their daily necessities and few luxuries that even their parents never dreamt off. They care

[7]See http://business.outlookindia.com/article.aspx?263508.

less if they have to work odd hours, without a break and away from their families in alien cities and countries. Similarly, young nuclear families with large outstanding loans of their car, housing etc., want to quickly earn more and fall prey to anti-WLB emotions. Unless the mindset changes take place where taking time off to attend sick parents or 4 days of outing every alternate month is not considered lack of commitments towards job, the situation will remain the same.

How can organisation enable their people?

There are many good ideas, many best practices and actions that the organisation can adapt to support WLB initiatives. The challenge is to find the appropriate ones and get convinced that such actions will not hamper work productivity and business results.

A well balanced employee is a gem for the firm in the long term. He manages his time so well that he does not let the job suffer thus needing less supervision. 'You finish your homework then can go out to play,' is an incentive parents always offer to their children. This incentive encourages the child to do her work with a lot of self-interest. Similarly, if the organisation allows the WLB incentives, work will be done faster, better and in a more congenial environment. I firmly believe this.

Let us look at the practices, rules and technology that organisation may adopt to help employees find time and impetus to balance their work life. There are several options that many good firms have started to offer their employees. We will list some of them for considerations.

Flexible work hours: Options like flexitime, where you decide when to start and end your working hours of the day is very useful. Many people, especially women with responsibilities of tender children, ageing parents can benefit from this flexibility of choice.

Part-time working: This feature allows employees to work either part-time everyday or few days a week at a lower emoluments level. Not only can it help employees attend to personal responsibilities such as finishing studies, but can also help employers to hire critical resources needed only for a short span of time.

Job sharing: In the work place, there would be days when one person has fewer loads and someone else more. The less loaded person, instead of whiling away his time can be asked to do job-sharing to help the other more loaded colleague.

Sabbatical: Allowing employees to take sabbaticals (taking unpaid time off for few months or a year) to undertake short courses, do community work or just take a long fun tour is another good possibility.

Use technology extensively: Many organisations allow employees performing certain job roles to work from home locations. Called tele-working (working remotely) or home working, this idea is great but requires maturity both from the organisation as well as the employee to make it effective. Further, it is now possible to use low cost broadband connections for desk top video and voice communication to ensure that the productivity is not compromised. Even if the employer with multiple offices in the same city allows employees to work from an office location that is closer to his / her home irrespective of where the rest of the team is located, the advantages are enormous.

Allow career breaks: Some of the traditional organisations[8] in India had this feature of three months of paid furlough leave after every 7 years of active service. Such leave can be utilised to undertake short career breaks to try activities of personal interest. One could accumulate this over two seven years periods and take leave at half pay for nearly one year.

Virtual work place: New age companies are increasingly encouraging Virtual Workplaces and employee mobility. Instead of attending meetings face-to-face they encourage telephonic bridges to enable multiple participants log in at one time and conduct meetings over phone.

Collaborative workplace: Facilities such as team rooms on the internet enables time delayed collaboration and also facilitates sharing of information for effective work output.

The future of work Culture is changing

Greater ownership and personal responsibility towards assigned work in a supervision less environment is a reality. Devices like mobile

[8]Tata Steel had this feature till the late 90s.

phones and internet enables and equips organisations to access employees' talent 24×7 rather than an 8 hour work day thus making conventional workplace redundant. At the same time physically present team based activities foster sense of one-ness amongst otherwise mobile workforce. In fact many work groups regularly hold pre-determined interaction to bring people together at a common location and then let them work remotely for the rest of the week.

What will it lead us to?

On one hand such policies and features give greater flexibility to employees to choose their work hours and work location, but also nudge them to stretch their work day at home with no finishing hour. The onerous will lie on the employees themselves to suitably apportion time slots for work and for personal needs. While giving too little work out remotely or misusing this flexibility will invite the employer's wrath, being glued to the laptop and mobile phone all the time would mean serious imbalance in their personal life. The choice is certainly on the employees themselves to neither misuse this flexibility nor get entrapped into a 24-hour work schedule in this bargain.

As an owner, employer or higher up in the hierarchy in the pecking order, we have a responsibility to cajole the employee to take necessary steps for their work life balance by giving them support, freedom and making them fearless[9] when they embrace this path. More than 60 per cent of the professional accepted in a recent survey that they find imbalance between their personal and professional lives. As result of which their performance at work and long term commitments did suffer. Work life imbalance is leading to stress, early burn out and depression in most cases. In extreme ones even cardiac ailment and failure were also reported. Organisations, especially the leading ones who have always remain in the forefront of employee reforms; encourage several work life balance initiatives some of which are discussed in the book. Every employee who is also a manager must bring change in the culture whichever level he or she belongs too.

The industrial revolution proved that in factories better working conditions, improved hygiene and several other improvements helped

[9]The essence of the Hindi word अभय (abhay) is not adequately captured in the English word fearless.

in improving productivity, less rejection and employee unrest. For the modern day service-led economy, work life balance is at the same stage where manufacturing companies were nearly hundred years ago. Studies have proved that this is a burning problem most companies are grappling with. In case the work life imbalance is not arrested and key individuals suffer then the company will loose more than the individual. Consider the CEO collapsing in between major shareholder meetings and the impact it will bring on the share prices!

Any organisation cannot just have some good 'golfing' policies for the inhabitant of corner office and for the rest a different one. The organisation has to have something similar and equitable for floor boys to directors. It must create a conducive climate for helping everyone work towards a balance work and life priorities. Organisation should undertake suggestive as well as prescriptive approach for its employees. While it can prescribe the employee to consume their annual leave, give holiday on their birthdays and of their spouse or children, it can also suggest a good vacation package by tying up with hotel chains seeking good discounts in lieu of their patronage of giving business when the employees stay as guest during work trips.[10] Organisations would indirectly gain from these initiatives in several ways. The most important amongst them is loyalty and dedication, creativity and capability.

Organisations like IBM, Merck, Deloitte & Touche, Google and other silicon valley start ups are known to promote free time, flexi-working and derive many significant creative outputs that a traditional mindset could not by chaining employees to their email boxes and long and odd-hour conference calls. Other benefits include increased individual productivity, accountability and commitment, better teamwork and communication. All this lead to improved morale, lower attrition, lower training and hiring cost and lower stress levels.

[10]Some leading companies in India have done this very effectively. It acts as incentives for employees to travel out because bulk rates are negotiated for say 1,000 room nights by the corporation for all its leisure travel of employees. Holiday homes in select destinations by major Public sector units, banks, etc., are good example for inducing employees to taking a break. These are small investments but help WLB efforts a lot.

Employees on the other hand tend to gain a balance in their daily life, increased work satisfaction, improved relationships both at work and family life. Less stress increases their chances of remaining disease free and a longer life span.

Some recommended actions

1. Create suitable training programmes to the employees on Work life Balance.
2. Use online, classroom webcasts as well as email campaign to build awareness and cascade the appreciation amongst employees. Use senior managers to respect and articulate the WLB advantage not just lip service or a runtime activity that is forced by HR department from time to time. All such message should be for work life balance, not one at the cost of other. Remember our two-leg example. The message should be like, 'We need to improve our business performance and our life performance together!'
3. There should be a sponsor from amongst the senior leadership team, several work life balance champions, role models and coaches from within the organisation. Select and train the trainer(s) programme to have more number of people available to cascade this initiative. HR professionals, trainers, members of the work-life team, and interested participants can form part of the trainee pool. Train even the volunteer family members of the employees who can be far more effective as a trainer than the employees themselves. It will also make the employees family aware of the seriousness of the organisation towards this step. Jeeva in one of his similar initiatives invited the spouses also to attend his workshop and it was phenomenal success. A spouse or close family a member can act as an in-house buddy who will encourage the employee to implement the commitment he/she had taken in this direction.
4. Publish newsletter, wall paper, cascade success stories, take interviews of employee parents, spouse or children to find what improvement he or she has got after the adoption of this programme.

5. Sustain and measure results, don't expect quick wins and short term results. Popularise the process and achievements as much as possible.

Summary of Key Themes

1. Organisations have to create an environment that facilitates work life balance.
2. Several actions as listed above are required to be undertaken. But this is not an exhaustive list.
3. A well balanced employee is a long term asset to the organisation and all the problems of attrition, lack of teaming, and unethical practices can be controlled by creating the right environment that supports work life balance.
4. Several best practice ideas can be adopted by the organisation to encourage employees making efforts and commitment towards their work life balance.
5. Creating a pool of champions, WLB trainers which may include some of the interested family members as well is a great idea to pursue implementation in the organisation beyond just lip service.
6. Various means of communications can be used to publish this idea across the organisation through newsletters, emails, mail cast/web cast or just showing running video in the cafeteria on WLB will help.

CHAPTER NINE

Message to Millennial GENERATION

The world, especially developing countries like India, is passing through a unique phenomenon. The millennial generation is swamping the society, work place and institutions. Recent spurt of growth, supporting family and dotting parents have led the new generations also called GenY or millennial generation to believe that world is just there to grab faster, easier and sooner. But the reality may belie their dream when they face the real world. Success without hard work often deceives them, jobs without skills even further and relationship without commitment seals them all. Every rejection, failure and disappointment leaves them empty without any hope. Some try to resort to short cuts and make their life even more complicated. For them the essence of what the life is all about and how it should be lived in balanced way is far more important than those who have learnt some of the lessons the hard way. The constrained generations of which their parents belonged were less disappointed when they were deprived of the new goodies. But the new generation may feel bad when they seem to lag behind and therefore undergo depression. They must practice some of the principles mentioned in the book right from early days before it becomes too late.

There are certain unique situations for this generation most of them born around or after 1990. They have new found energy in the body, smartness, and ease with technology gadgets, hormonal rush and of course pocket money. They are optimistic to the core, usually short term thinker, some of them high achievers who also care for environment, society and their health at the same time. They think that they have the potential to be great and they are probably right. Yet they need to learn from past mistakes of the earlier generation and be careful to see the larger picture of life, which is beyond self-gratification, self-delusion and self-aggrandisement. If they don't learn from their earlier generation's experience then they will have disappointments soon enough and cause self-inflicted injuries that would be difficult to heal.

Like it happened in the past, the parents of this generation also have limited tools in their tool chest to deal with them. Parents are awestruck with their children's technical prowess, ability to get better jobs and penchant for quality of life. Parents are handicapped to peep in their son's or daughter's mind and know very little as to what is going on in the chat sessions behind closed doors of their bedrooms.

Why this world is does not understand them? Why is the world so difficult place to be and why can't things happen now? These are and many other questions in the minds of millennial generations. In this chapter I will try to address some of their questions and suggest some answers that they may try. Please note I am not prescribing any solution or guaranteeing its success as I firmly believe in experimenting by practitioners and only then getting convinced. Without making any preamble let me add some prescription especially for this generation over and above what we have discussed already.

Don't blame the past: Well if you are having the problem then it is not the creation of your parents, managers, friends or government. May be the problem is genuine but there is no point blaming any one. If you can then try to navigate, solve or eradicate with limited capability or circle of influence that you may have. For example don't blame your parents for not sending you to Ivy League college because they could not afford the big ticket fee. Instead of remaining illiterate or less educated throughout your life, find another college that you can afford from student loan. After all, the entire world is not made up only of alumni from premier colleges or institutes. If your manager has not promoted you every alternate year don't blame him/her or the organisation for your career stagnation, find another, he is not the only manager or this is not the only company to work with. In personal relationship if someone rejects your proposal don't rush with blade or acid bottle or jump from 9th floor, world is made of several billion people you too will find a decent and better one. There is not point insisting of that job, company or person and getting angry when you don't get it.

You are not a child any longer: When a child demands something, the parents rush to meet it, partly due to love, mostly because they can afford and largely to allow the child his or her happiness. Now this behaviour continues as you go past your teens to adulthood. Unfortunately, your employer is not your parent who would sacrifice to please you. They have a business to run and you will feel disappointed after some time as you will not get regular positive strokes like promotions, raise, accolades or awards every month or year. Now you will have to reconcile that there are extraneous factors on which the manager may not have any control, for example spend cut due to poor performance of the firm in the market. Unfortunately some may look unfair to you but that is the real world and you must know how to face it. Even God has not created everyone as equal; some are tall, some short and some fat, fair or ugly. So accept what comes your way.

Manage Expectations: Most of us feel hurt when our expectations are not met. Many youngsters has similar predicament in their growing up years. They feel that they could do no wrong, fail in no exam and hence could not be denied any raise at work just because they are discharging their responsibilities immaculately. But when you realise that the external factors could play spoilt sport in some situation you will be calmer and feel better. You should stop expecting a promotion every two years, success in every interview or double increments every year. When you approach these situations with open mind you will be surprised with success and less disappointed when rejected.

Most of us are subjected to defend the aura of inflated expectation from people and organisation around us. Many start believing that rewards or acceptance are their birth right. So they retaliate and remorse when rejected. There is no need for either. Just move on to wait for the next opportunity.

Understand and deliver your value: Every recent generation is likely to be more informed, better equipped than their predecessors like Operating system or mobile hand set. Even though, many may not be dramatically superior to the earlier ones like their seniors or parents. In work you may be more educated than your manager, at home earning better than your elder brother, but hold on before throwing your superiority syndrome to them. You must understand that they were like you few years ago and you will be like them few years later. A new mobile phone will have a higher megapixel camera than the one belonging to an earlier generation but both of them are used to click photographs! A box camera which snapped your childhood photographs is dearer to your mom than your 13 megapixel one you bought recently. So respect her emotions and don't laugh or force her to like your gadget. Likewise if you cannot become useful to the organisation, acceptable to peers and loved by your team, it is immaterial if you have superior capabilities.

Forget, forgive and move on: At your age you may run into arguments, someone may cheat you or walk over. You can not fix the entire world and make it a life long mission to reform all such wrongs or people who perpetrated them. What you could do instead is to forget, forgive and just move to the new task, taking up a new opportunity on new day in front of you.

Before asking try giving: So far you have been asking for things from your parents, elders, teachers and rest of the world. They were happy to give those things to you but now the clock has turned. Understand your responsibilities are now to give back more than what you have got. Some of you may already have a job, so find ways how you can give more than you have got. In relationships, worry less about your demands but more about how you can meet your partner's needs. In your family, make sure you are now an active contributing member and not a passive spectator. For society, work as an element of positive change and do not resist it.

Surprise everyone: You with your clean and innovative mind can make a lot of difference in the society. We routinely witness such mass euphoria when some public event happens and the youth congregates with candle light protest. But go beyond protest to do something at a scale what you have in your command. Instead of cribbing about bureaucratic hurdles a 2009 batch IAS officer[1] built a 100 km road that would link Manipur with Nagaland and Assam by inviting donation from people using a Facebook post. Well you, also can surprise the world with your new innovative ways.

Will you?

Summary of Key Themes

1. The new generation also called millennial generation is the new hope of the society
2. They need to be careful while choosing options for their life and change their approach.
3. Some suggestions
   a. Don't blame your parents, managers, friends, society or government.
   b. Find solution to the problem at hand
   c. Become responsible adult to accept limitation of life not a child that gets everything
   d. Manage Expectations of others and also with yourself
   e. Understand and deliver your value in every interaction
   f. In case of disappointment or conflict forget, forgive and move on
   g. Before asking try giving in your relationship
   h. Surprise everyone with your clean and innovative mind

Finally be active contributor not a passive spectator.

[7]See http://business.outlookindia.com/article.aspx?263508.

CHAPTER TEN

Simply, Safety, STRONGLY

Be brave! Be strong! Be fearless!

—Swami Vivekananda (1863–1902)

You may wonder what these three seemingly unconnected words are doing here. This book is about how to make the most out of the limited life we have. It was important to define what life is all about and what its ultimate purpose is. We examined several tools, tricks and lessons from those who have understood this unique subject far more in detail. The time has come to take action simply, safely and smartly. These three words encapsulate the overall guiding principles.

Simplify things to make your life free from confusion and complexity. This has been discussed at several places in earlier chapters. But this needs to be elaborated once again. When you simplify your approach you will feel less burdened, and save time and effort that can be utilised in those pursuits that are more useful to you. So leave no efforts when the opportunity comes to make your life simple. Choose simple gadgets, simple meals, simple relationships and simple ways to lead your life. You will have to weigh every time options come in front of you, and then chose the simplest amongst them. You will enjoy freedom from managing too many things and devote your time to other activities that you may enjoy. We have broached up the advantages of simplicity from work life balance perspective at several places in the book and this is one principle that we must adopt as a first step to change our life course.

Safety is one discipline that seems to have been relegated to the background in the modern age. Live your life following principles of safety so that you survive longer and are happier. Avoid taking unnecessary risk, the examples of which you see every day, from crossing a busy street with cell phone earphone on, driving after couple of drinks, to putting money in riskier investments promising unbelievable returns. Consider the finality of your choice going wrong, for example, if the bus does not slow down or the firm promising to double your money disappears! Driving in a cris-cross or zig-zag fashion at 150 kmph will surely someday leave you without an arm, a leg, or even your life. The same is true when high profile executives take risky jobs in a company or invest in a extra-marital relationship and end up regretting later. The point is not to discourage you from taking risk but, the inability to visualise the outcome is a problem. Remember—don't try your luck too hard to test it to the extent that one day it gives up.

We started with a premise that all of us have a limited time and therefore if we want to achieve more, and fill our life with a variety of experiences then we have to save time and energy and above all, our life. For doing this we need to be efficient and save time. This is the theme that will demand us to use technology, many of which may have unforeseen safety issues. For example your personal data, password and privacy may be compromised when you are shouting in a busy airport or mall talking to your investment advisor, or typing furiously on your laptop or smart phone. Someone may be watching, overhearing or trying to do the mischief. In case you work in other countries and travel to places which may be unknown then safety of life, money or reputation are also to be considered. We routinely read in newspapers instances where people lost their life money or reputation when they were not cautious enough. Don't cap your life for a short-lived pleasure, thrill or just try things such as drugs, or be associated with dubious people without understanding the consequences. This principle is to ensure that we be aware of the unnecessary risk and its consequences before taking our major decisions in life and prevent from getting trapped after doing something wrong.

Finally, for doing all this, walking the path that you have chosen will need enormous inner strength. Be **Strong** as you will have many distractions, many temptations and peer pressure when you chart out a different course than what others are following. Vivekananda, a revered saint of our times rightly tells us to beware of compromises. He says, 'I do not mean that you are to get into antagonism with anybody, but you have to hold on to your own principles in weal or woe and never adjust them to others "fads" thought the greed of getting supporters.'[1] This will require you to be strong and hold on to your principles. You are embarking to transform your life which will not happen if you don't possess the strength of conviction, power of dedication and spirit of persistence. Unless you are strong enough to resist the temptations and ensure that you would not deviate from the principles you have decided to adopt nothing will ever be achieved. So go out and change your life you will need all of these virtues in this journey to **Live** Unlimited happiness, accomplishments, satisfactions and gain unlimited love and respect.

[1]See http://www.vivekananda.org/quotes.aspx accessed 18092013.Ed: most website references do not provide access dates. Please take a call on whether to query the author for the same or not.

CHAPTER ELEVEN

Tools, Techniques and TEMPLATES

Here are some of the tools and instruments that will help us in assimilating of our efforts for achieving work life balance.

A. WLB quiz: Test how balanced you are?

Please assign 1 to 5 scores for each of these questions, 1 being least applicable and 5 being most likely.

1. Do you work more than 10 hours every day? ☐
2. Do you feel frustrated and feel guilty about non-work responsibilities? ☐
3. Do you miss you commitments such as reaching in nephews, cousin, close friends wedding anniversary or birthdays. ☐
4. Do you drive or travel more than 90 minutes every day both ways in commuting or during the course of your work? ☐
5. Do you often skip your lunch break or rush to finish lunch in 15 minutes or eat lunch/junk food at 3:30pm when you are most hungry? ☐

6. Do you miss out on quality time with your family and friends because of a work deadline? ☐
7. Do you think negatively about work with regards to your personal life? ☐
8. You do not spend any time during the week in solicitude thinking about yourself. ☐
9. You are worried about your work place issues, politics or new rules. ☐
10. You are always tired or depressed, feel suffocated or loose temper often. ☐
11. Do you spend more and more time outside of work on work-related issues? ☐
12. Do you lose sleep often on work issues or get up in the middle of the night? ☐
13. Do you feel rushed with your every day schedule all the time? ☐
14. Do you feel as confused and lost about what you are achieving in your life? ☐
15. Do you skip exercises and events like watching movies/shows often? ☐
16. Do you feel stressed, exhausted, tired and burnt out most of the time? ☐
17. You do not have time to spend with close friends. ☐
18. You can't remember when you went on a vacation. ☐
19. You have several personal affairs/responsibilities that need attention, but where is the time? ☐
20. You feet like taking time off between two assignments, the last one was too draining but the bosses did not allow you to. ☐
21. Despite the fact that your have keen interest in writing, reading

books, painting, theater or singing, it has been a long time since you have indulged in one. ☐

22. You have missed so many family events that you have lost count of them. ☐
23. You are always overburdened due to several family commitments and responsibilities in terms of your time, activities as well as finances. ☐
24. You were better off when you were in your earlier job/stage of life, e.g., when you were a student. ☐
25. You feel there is no one to look up to for advice or guidance on work life related issues. ☐

While scoring be honest, and at the same time do not be too critical. If your score is above:

- 100, the work place is not for you, change it now
- 70 but less than 100, you need to seek change in work style and priorities act on various prescription of the book seriously and immediately
- 40 but less than 70, the balance is slipping, time to take action
- 25 but less than 40, you need to be aware that WLB is a constant struggle not just reading a book and answering a few quizzes. So better be sensitive and proactive to walk the path and take efforts and guidance continuously.
- If the score is 25, then you are a role model of work life balance. Just do a double check if you answered them honestly and not just to show a good report!

This set of questions is just to take the dip stick test of where you are of your journey to achieve balance in life. There is not passing or fail marks. It may be good idea to answer these questions along with your close buddy or spouse, someone who is not afraid to call out your failings. It is always better to have an unbiased but totally dedicated individual who can be a corrective light for you. Some times you may find it in a mentor or guru who can chasten you from time to time in days when you are running too fast or going too slow. Respect their inputs as they will help you guide the changes towards a well balance life towards the path of Ananda.

B. Define your balanced life goals for the next 5 years

(Balanced Goals /for (Next 5 years)

Artha Financial	Dharma Duty/ Responsibility	Kama Pleasure	Mokshya Self-actualisation, spiritual
Define your Goal			
Define Your current state			
Prioritise key areas			
Draft a plan of action		–	

C. Work Life Balance: a typical Day Plan

A well balanced day must have time allotted for the following activities:

- Personal chores (washing, brushing, etc.) 02 hours
- Work including commuting 11 hours
- Sleep 07 hours
- Family 02 hours
- Self-development, exercise, yoga, reading etc. 02 hours

In addition, during the weekends the extra 10–12 hours available should be apportioned as:

- Finishing transactions such as Bank, Utility bill etc. 04 hours
- Family 05 hours
- Friends 02 hours
- Self-development (study, spirituality, getting mentoring) 05 hours

Plan a typical day and review it at night if you have been able to drive it the way you wanted to. Thank the lord irrespective of how the day has gone by and pray before going to bed and as soon as you get up and seek blessings.

As soon as you get up:

1. Don't jump out of your bed.
2. Move your toes and heel in circular motion.
3. Get up and keep yourself in sitting posture for some time for about 20 seconds.
4. Then, observe your palms together by joining them like a cup for a minute every day and recite this shloka.

Karagre Vasate Lakshmi Karmadhye Saraswati
Karmule Tu Govindaha Prabhaate Karadarshanam[1]

5. Rub your palms lightly over your face.
6. Observe which nostril is active and breathing, touch that ground with that feet first
7. Take a clockwise circle in all direction while praying to the lord, your parents and guru.

All this should take about 2–3 minutes. This will make the first good beginning of the day. When you pray just seek from your lord to give you good thinking, good opportunities, enthusiasm to do face the day and overall peace. Don't ask or beg any thing worldly in the morning.

[1]कराग्रे वसते लक्ष्मी करामद्ये सरस्वती , करमूले तू गोविन्दः प्रभाते करदर्शनम Translated it means We should observe our palm every morning as it is the palm that has Lakshmi on its front portion, Saraswati in the middle and Goving at its root.

Thank the supreme power for giving you yet another day to live in the wonderful world that it is You may be down on some days, ill or have had a bad night for some reason. Don't break the routine. You will not see results next day, but over several days when you follow that routine. Prayers have great power to protect us. But you have to have faith and repeat it for several days, moths or years to start realising your desire.

What is the ideal time to get up? Well I would not say that you get up at 4:30 or 5 am as advised by saints and sages of the ancient times. Perhaps with all the new age routine, commute etc., it is not always possible to wake up early. All I suggest that whatever time you normally wake up, try half an hour early and then after 6 months another half an hour early. You will be surprised to notice the change in your daily routine and abilities to manage things. In case of Jeeva, when he started to get up at 530 (his usual habit was 7 am) he found so much of extra time for morning yoga, prayer etc., and also helped him to beat the traffic. Once this routine gets drawn up, you will notice that you lounge to go to bed early and don't waste time in flicking channels on unnecessary news or reality shows!

D. Must spend time for Meditation, Yoga and Breathing exercise

What should be our exercise / yoga routine? My advice for exercise or yoga is not for building body muscles or toning up the muscular strength. For all that a professional gym instructor should be taken. My recommendation is neither for nor against all these practices. In certain types of professions[2] where body requires more rigorous discipline such planned exercises are necessary. Yes in order to achieve our work life balance a simple yoga exercise regime is recommended. There are many popular yoga process teachers and guru, any one of them would be good enough for us to follow. Author has found merit in adopting Nam-yog[3] practices where by

[2]Sports persons, security personnel, dance, drama and movie professionals.

[3]Nam-yoga teachings are available by writing to nam_yog@yahoo.com.

following a routine this routine for 20-25 minutes lets both body and mind rejuvenated.

E. Start the day with simple breathing exercise and yoga

Pranayam, the breathing exercise is the simplest and most useful of all types of yoga. Combining prayer, mediation and pranayam can help achieve multiple objectives of healthy body, mind and spirit.

1. Then just breathe normally and focus your attention on the inhalation and exhalation. The pronunciation of word Om (or any other according to your belief) when inhaling (pran) and exhaling (apana) is a good practice that creates healthy vibrations.
2. While sitting down in the cross legged position is recommended, in case some of have discomfort, start while sitting in a un-arm chair.
3. With hands folded in a namaskar mudra, lips as if smiling, inhale deeply and then exhale. Repeat for 3 minutes.
4. Continue sitting with hands straight on knees and index finger and thumb making a ring. Just exhale and make an impact on the back bone by navel (nabhi). Practice time 3 minutes. This step should be practiced only after 5 hours of meals and should be done on empty stomach. This is also known as Kapalbhati Kriya.
5. Inhale from your left nostril and exhale from the right nostril and vice-versa very slowly and deeply, and then repeat it. In case one feels giddiness he should stop and start again after rest. Practice time—3 minutes. It is also called Anulom vilom.
6. Close both your ears with the help of both of your thumbs. Take a deep breath with and exhale while pronouncing OM. Practice 3 times.
7. Finally end the process by giving Thanks to God for giving yet another wonderful day ahead of you and pray that he gives you the necessary strength to face the world.

It is recommended that guidance from a trained practitioner be taken who can demonstrate the process well. Some popular TV channels do show these processes, or you search on internet and adopt from them.

What to do after the yoga practice? All this would take around 30 minutes. After this one can walk or jog and does some fitness exercise depending upon the interest and time available. Once done, one should finish the daily chores like bath, breakfast and getting ready for work.

F. How do we behave during the day?

- While driving on the road keep chanting any prayer that you may like. Alternatively humming a nice song that gives positive feeling can be equally good.
- Don't worry if someone drives rash and goes ahead of you, the total distance covered is the same, and a few minutes will not make much difference.
- Start early to beat the traffic.
- Perform every action to save time, resources and with efficiency.

Don't drag or the meetings unnecessarily.

- Save time, electricity other forms of energy as well other natural resources.
- Try to be the 'green' employee who is non-polluting and spreads smiles and happiness all around.
- Add smile in the life of co workers specially the one who is at the lower ladder. Appreciate their small efforts, thank them for their service and guide them to do something better in their life.
- Stay away from bitching, back biting and making disparaging remarks towards the colleagues.
- If praise come your way handle with humility, if criticism comes take it in your stride, improve if you are convince of the suggestion, disregard if it is done with ulterior motive.
- Finish your assigned work, do something over and above what is assigned. Yet if you have free time use the online learning resources too get your skills enhanced.
- Avoid browsing social networking sites and other socially unacceptable sites during office hours.

G. Evening actions

Evening is the family time. Talking with family, being of help in solving day to day problems and helping children in their studies helps to improve the bondage. Also sharing as well as asking some interesting events about the happening of the office will make everyone know what are you doing and what problems you face in your day to day life. You need not discuss every bit of office gossip or all activities but some key ones will help.

Our protagonist Jeeva was not in the habit of sharing these details, considering it too complex and would cause tension. His family did not know what challenges he was facing at job or what kind of turmoil he is going through. The family could have given him objective advice and would have encouraged him to address those problems.

If time permits after or before dinner, take short stroll in the near by park, go to the nearby market to buy vegetables, milk or whatever or just say hello to the neighbors!

H. Before falling asleep

Just before you fall asleep, sit down on the bed pray with folded hands to thank the God almighty for giving us the beautiful life and the wonderful day. Reflect on some of the weaknesses or errors that crept in and pray that God will help us overcome them tomorrow. We cannot say that all days will be trouble free but you will find slowly if you observe this behaviour you will find gradual improvement and calming down effect happening to you.

Finally, pray to God before falling asleep.

I. Suggested food intake

Proper food intake enables us to meet the daily challenges of life, live a longer and healthier without dependence till the last day. Food also adds to our mental well being. It is no secret that eating a balance natural food makes us pursue any dream that we may have as we are healthy and fit. If we are ill, the people around us become more troubled than the person himself. Jeeva realised this and changes his eating and health care habits drastically. A balanced food will balance your life style. Eat good breakfast, lighter lunch and frugal dinner. It is said that eat breakfast like a king, lunch of a commoner and dinner as pauper. Some suggested portions in day are as follows:[4]

- Carbohydrate: Bread, Cereal, Rice etc., Less than 6 servings
- Antioxidants / Vitamins Fruit 2 to 4 servings
- Green and leafy Vegetable 3 to 5 servings
- Protein Milk, Yogurt and Cheese 2 to 3 servings
- Meat, Poultry, Fish, Dry Beans and Nuts 2 to 3 servings
- Fats, Oils and Sweets: Use as little as possible.
- Eat only when you feel hungry and always eat in small quantities.
- Never fill your stomach and overeat.

J. Draw your work life balance sheet:

Ascertain how you are wasting your time everyday

1. No of junk work email: (___) X 1 minutes =(______)Minutes / day
2. Unsolicited Personal emails: (_____) X 1 minutes = (_________) Minutes / day
3. Browsing Social networking sites, (_____) X 10 minutes = (_____) Minutes/ day
4. Marketing Calls received: (_____) X 1 minutes = (_____)Minutes / day
5. Calls made that were prolonged: (_____) X 1 minutes = (____) Minutes / day *
6. Time in conference attended for more than 1 hour: = (___) Minutes / day*
7. Number of meetings attended beyond one hour: (_) X 30 min= (_)Minutes / day

[4]A proper advice with dietician depending upon the age and other requirements should be made. These are just indicative.

8. Travel time per day beyond one hour: = (_____)Minutes / day
   A Add any other time wasters per day = (_____) Minutes/ day
9. Total time minutes wasted per day Sum 1-8 (_____) Minutes
10. Total days wasted per year Total Value Srl.9 X 250 days = days
11. Number of days away per month, (_____) X 12 = days

The number of days in line 10 and 11 will give you an idea of how much you are wasting your life on meaningless pursuits.

*Most meetings or conference calls that go beyond 60 minutes cannot hold the attention of the participants. Work place discipline demands chair of the meetings to force strict agenda and monitor unnecessary cross talk, diverting the issue, hogging the lime light or indulging in take-off participation.

k. Understand your abilities and traits through metaphors

Human learning is largely facilitated through examples and action though associations. The idea is that if each one of us identifies oneself with one or two of these metaphors, we can understand our hidden abilities and traits. Having a good understanding of oneself is sure recipe of achieving success by choosing right job, career and work style. These metaphorical objects can help us unearth our hidden desires and capabilities that can help identify the jobs that we will excel in.

Over 200 participants in diverse batches across Indian Subcontinent for over 5 years were asked to relate and articulate their deep buried desires and abilities using these metaphors. Their unanimous feedback was that it helped. They consequently started to look for job roles that manifested these traits. Years later most gave positive feedback of finding their true likes. Many of these metaphors came from the participants of the Return to life workshop themselves. These participants offered unique and interesting explanations as to why they feel they are able to identify with a particular metaphor, animal or object.

By all means this is not an exhaustive list you can choose objects beyond them if you wish. But do understand what these are revered for and how are they related with your abilities and traits. Upon your feedback we will enhance this list in future editions.

Type of animal or natural object	What does it signify	Relevant in modern context	Key word
1 Dolphin	Playfulness, community living, Interactive and communicative helpful in distress	Social service, Communication	Playful
2 Fox	Opportunist, Contented, Excellent sensory perception. Playful with other foxes.Alert to the environment, adaptable beautiful well-groomed fur.	Sales, security services, Investigative journalism Strategist	Cunning
3 Beaver	Hard working, family oriented, cooperative and rarely fight, change locations to find adequate water, forest and seclusion	Dedicated worker, Protector and provider	Busy and work oriented
4 Owl	Powerful eyesight, almost 360 view even in dark. Quiet observer, can see their enemies ahead of time.	Strategists observers, Long range planners, Thinkers	Wise
5 Horse	Winning a race, focus attention	Project management	Winner
6 Dog	Loyalty to master,	Audit and protector intelligence gathering	Dedicated
7 Elephant	Slow but carries great load, team player,	Project management,	Load carrier

Type of animal or natural object	What does it signify	Relevant in modern context	Key word
	playful, useful even after its death		
8 Tiger	Leader, disciplinarian,	Leadership roles	King
9 River	Flow, constant change, nourishing	New, opportunities sales and marketing job, consulting	Flow
10 Cloud	Wondering, rain carrying, useful	Consultants, advisors	Brings joy
11 Tree	Shades, fruit, environment friendly	Delivery team, Located at a place	Tall and useful
12 Flower	Beauty, fragrance	Show business	Beauty

L. How self-aware you are?[5]

1. ___ I know what I am capable of in terms of my abilities, talents, and interests.
2. ___ I am able to devise my own short-term and long term goals
3. ___ I am able to gather resources and necessary support to achieve them

[5]Some questions were Adapted from, http://content.cellt.org/diglib/1-18/SelfAssessmentOfStrengthsAndWeaknesses.pdf

4. ___ I can manage my time, tasks, and resources well
5. ___ I can assess progress of my personal life.
6. ___ I am willing to reassess my goals and redirect them
7. ___ I am aware of my own feelings.
8. ___ I also aware of other people's feelings and respect them
9. ___ I am able to freely participate, cooperate and contribute in team activity.
10. ___ If situation arise I can lead team
11. ___ I can express personal feelings of care, respect, and support for others.
12. ___ I communicate with others with clarity and purpose.
13. ___ I present myself as being genuine, honest, and trustworthy.
14. ___ I am able to think independently.
15. ___ I am beginning to react and share on observations, thoughts and feelings.
16. ___ I maintain attention and focus to accomplish class and personal goals.
17. ___ I handle risk and challenge with courage.
18. ___ I take failure an opportunity to learn and take renewed effort to try again
19. ___ I know that criticism and praise are two sides of the same coin. I will neither get dejected or elated but accept them to improve myself.
20. ___ I am learning how to assess my person, process and performance.

Scores: 19–20: are your sure? You are one of the rare self-aware one.

16–18: You are very close on your path, keep moving.

12–15: better than average, make more efforts.

10–12: A lot is required to be done.

Less than 10: You may have lot to introspect to correct the situation.

M. Re Work your Life: Monitor your Progress

(Use scale of 1–5, 5 being most desirable)

Date of Resolution .... Name of the buddy to review......

Srl number	Suggested action	Current State	30 days later	60 days later	90 days later
1	Start managing you day using FLIP model				
2	Simplify your life by • Reduced Transaction overload • Speaking truth • Having fewer but solid relationship • Removing noise • Using technology judiciously				
3	Do not disrupt the pace of event often.				
4	Un-clutter your mind				
5	Think positive, Have fun				
6	Develop a helping attitude				
7	Just be yourself and don't punish it too much				

M. Re Work your Life: Monitor your Progress

(Use scale of 1–5, 5 being most desirable)

Date of Resolution .... Name of the buddy to review......

Srl number	Suggested action	Current State	30 days later	60 days later	90 days later
8	Stop procrastinating				
9	Live a day at a time				
10	Be a good human being				
11	Balance your life following the Middle path				
12	Balance Body, Mind and Soul				
13	Control your anger and dedicate to love.				
14	Have faith, trust and devotion				
15	Finally Realise yourself, attain freedom				

N. Some assorted FAQs on WLB

Lot of you will be impatient to exactly find answers to your situation. That is why these FAQs will help. You may be aware that these questions are like guidance for point to point journey hence would be limited in solving all the issues that you may have. But they will be a good pointer to start off with. If you end up not finding your answer to the question bugging your mind consult the author by sending a short email.

1. *I am very young and just turning 20. Does this philosophy any good for me?*

   WLB is meant to be practiced at all age irrespective. At your age the chances are you are finishing your study in few years time and want to take a path for your life. It is important to consider what you think are most important for life and whether they are worth considering important. You may need some bouncing off ideas with your parents, teachers, friends and life coach who can help clarify your goal a bit better. Your friends in your age group may be as ignorant as you so just don't depend solely on them.

   WLB will help you establish this very goal through the balancing of all the fourth facets of life as explained in Chapter 3. You may give more important for one or two at this stage but you cannot ignore the rest. Remember the three pillars of our life as discussed in chapter 4.

   A short answer, Yes I think so, you will be far better prepared if you start your life following a balanced approach so that you have little to un do later on and regret lesser.

2. *I just retired and have all the good trappings of life such as house, pension, and settled children; I guess I have nothing to take away now. Am I right?*

   Wrong, Absolutely. Granted that you have taken care of few steps that can lead your life in comfort but is the reason you came in the world? Just think about it. Your life is unique, no one knew who you were before you came. Would you like to remain as such after you leave the scene? It perhaps is time for giving back and making yourself closer to the needs of others. Would you enjoy eating, drinking and attending to mundane activities for the rest of your life? Would you be just happy doing nothing that you can be proud off? Think of it, you will find the answer.

3. *I am a young woman with multiple responsibilities. Job, young children and a family. WLB is good but I guess I don't have time to look through. May be I will try after 10-12 years.*

It will be rather late to put back the life on WLB track again. The modern generations have this problem due to nuclear family set up and constant struggle between career and family. This is more so for women as they have a dominant responsibility of the mother. My first take is asserting your option with the organisation to get you a role or job that helps you manage this period. Try out tele-working, part time assignment and roles that can allow you manage your time well. At the same time don't just try to address this problem all by yourself and sulk. Share and seek cooperation with the family, distribute, delegate and devise ways that can help you. Consider options to seek help of elders and advice if necessary. You must make a conscious effort.

4. *I am sure you are not serious about busy executives on high growth trajectory to adopt any of these principles. After all WLB will look funny amongst my high achievers circle. I think it should be for someone who is depressed and stagnated in his or her career. What do you say?*
All I can say that you seem to me like a guy who is walking happily looking at the beautiful sky over the cliff, not realising that a deep gorge is just awaiting you in the next steps. Living the life in the fast lane for approval of others and for others is a sure recipe for disaster. In fact you will achieve much more following these steps. Don't you rest your machine, oil and grease, let the engine cool down after a long run. Even a horse needs rest, rejuvenation and recreation after a race; you are just a human being. This approach will help you widen your contribution to the larger society than just to your self and your firm. As a matter of fact if you adopt this approach your contributions will be far greater than what you are doing it just now

I think you are the most suitable candidate for WLB, please adopt it.

5. *Let me tell you that I am in very comfortable job. I have no work, no pressure, live in campus like atmosphere so I don't think there is any reason to try this at all. Any comments?*
Doing nothing is not WLB. A true work life balance is living a life for a purpose for the larger goods to the society. You have plenty of time which you may be whiling away in useless gossips or fruitless activities. You are fortunate that you are not under stress due to long hours of work, commute time etc and have a

decent salary or income. But think of it what legacy you are going to leave behind for the larger society where you are a part of. You must give back to the world, something constructive, some happiness and something good that you can lay your name on and makes you feel proud. WLB is not a prescription of idling and doing nothing!

6. *I don't think this approach is good enough for me. Being a home maker saddled with growing up children ageing parents and demanding spouse there is very little left for me to balance. Yet I want to know if you think differently.*

   Yes, I do. The role of being a home maker is most coveted yet under appreciated. As a coach and strong believer in WLB, my suggestion to you to seriously adopt the WLB model for yourself too. Remember like the job outside in any organization, the work you do at home is just one part of your personality. Still you have to do something more and beyond to realise your full potential. You life is as gifted as any one else. As a first step you have to desire, decide, demand time and space for balancing your life. If you develop your will power and resolve that you want to live your life the way you want to realise it to its fullest potential, no one can stop you.

   Nigella Lawson's book, How to be a Domestic Goddess is a very useful one. It resurrects the importance of modern full-time home makers and mothers. Remember you like many other contemporary women (and some men) have chosen domesticity by choice rather than compulsion, so you must also achieve what you wish to in addition to being a home maker. There are several creative, entrepreneurial as well as part time job initiatives that you can do along side being a home maker. Don't do any of these for extra money as money making role your family has not assigned to you. Do them for your self-satisfaction and personal goal realisation. If you start doing them then you will never have to retire as it will be your work done from home at your will. Betty Friedan[6] says that housewives or home makers have same

[6]The Feminine Mystique by Betty Friedan Published by Laurel, 1984 ISBN 10: 0440324971 / ISBN 13: 9780440324973).

aspirations for autonomy and fulfillment as all other human beings (that is, men), they too have to have 'work life balance' that is not just having enough time to spend with the family, but your need and desire for educational and cultural activities, for involvement in community groups and or political activism.

Now that you understand what I am leading to, why not prepare your five year WLB plan as per the template given in chapter 11.B. I agree that majority of the prescription are for people who work for others but you have a better score for WLB because you can assert and get this far easily than others.

7. *I am rather surprised that you want me to drop off all my achievements for few unproven, unsure goals like 'self-actualization' 'giving back to society' etc. I am doing great, just became Deputy Chief Asst Vice President, I guess these ideas can wait, unless you want to suggest something differently.*

Accordingly to a recent *The Economist* report[7] title inflation is one of the ploys played by corporations as an alibi against not increasing your salary during the economic slow down. So whether it is the fluffy title that you recently acquired or bigger cabin, you remain the same. Will any of these bring more lasting self-achievement that we all talked about? If yes, do nothing but the chances are that your life is beyond the corporation where you work and you need to take charge if it, before it is too late.

I am a successful business person and I agree with some of your advice very well. But I am not convinced if one should do any thing without return. After all we do lots of good to people but what return do we get?

Most people who are well provided for suffer more than what strugglers have to do. Spending your life without giving back to society is like a tree that neither gives shelter nor fruit to anyone. The purpose of life is also to give back to society otherwise what you will do after just creating wealth for yourself and to your family, enjoying all the types of food and other pleasures or visiting all the places. You must leave a legacy behind for all those who have no direct relationship with you and this approach will help you.

[7]See http://www.economist.com/node/16423358?story_id=16423358&fsrc=nlw%7Chig%7C06-24-2010%7Ceditors_highlights

CHAPTER ELEVEN

Epilogue
IT IS YOUR LIFE . . . YOU MUST ACTUALISE

You may wonder where Jeeva disappeared in between the story.

This story was never meant to be his biography. It never intended to tell how Jeeva achieved his work life balance, but to tell the lessons he learnt, the thoughts that inspired him, which his readers, friends and colleagues could use. It is easy to preach when you are not subjected to the situation, but it is difficult to decide when you are stuck in it as you have the responsibility to walk the talk. These lessons and thoughts are not only 'to-dos' for the readers, but as much for Jeeva himself.

He wanted to give back some wisdom from his pain to help others enjoy happiness in their life.While the desire to balance his life happened to Jeeva due to a life-threatening situation, he also had to persistently act on the steps that he had envisaged.

Remember, the best steps are those that we decide to take ourselves.

It was tough for him to realise that he could not transform overnight. He had to slowly but steadily traverse the path he had carved out for himself.

He was no Siddhartha or like many other greats who could renounce everything to spend their life pursuing just one thought. He desired to balance his life and achieve its purpose while being useful to the larger community. He also loved his family and was willing to subsume his desire to be together with them. He was an ordinary human being who craved for pleasure as well.

It was the action phase of the story where he merged in his own words, trying to live up to them, syllable by syllable.

For each prescriptive step there was an action that had been taken by him to see if it worked. I am certain if they brought positive changes in Jeeva's life, it can happen in yours as well.

So, you may not see him often in the text in the later chapters, but you can feel that he was just hiding behind the words trying to implement his own ideas and tell you…

'You too can!'

Has he completely transformed himself? The answer is *no.* But, he is still trying.

For him, living his life unlimited has just begun.

By following these actions, yours will too.

Life is limited … live unlimited!

Bibliography and ADDITIONAL RESOURCES

Selected web sites

- For individuals:
- Write to author on itsm.ssdubey@gmail.com to seek free personal advice and mentoring on variety of subject such as work life balance, career moves, success in job interviews etc.
- Self inventory; http://www.pcusa.org/prep4min/pdf/self_inventory.pdf
- For employers:
- http://www.worklifebalance.org/
- http://www.workfoundation.com/difference/e4wlb.aspx

Books, articles:

- 'Work-Life Balance Doing It Right And Avoiding The Pitfalls', Jim Bird. *Employment Relations Today*, Autumn 2006, vol. 33, no. 3, Wiley Periodicals, Inc.
- David Keirsey and Marilyn Bates, *Please Understand Me: Character and Temperament Types* (Prometheus Nemesis, 1984).

- Dr Kerr Inkson, *Understanding Careers: The Metaphors of Working Lives* (Hardcover) (Sage Publications, Inc, July 7, 2006).
- Robert A. Palmatier, *Speaking of Animals: Dictionary of Animal Metaphors* (Hardcover), (Greenwood Press, 30 April. 1995).